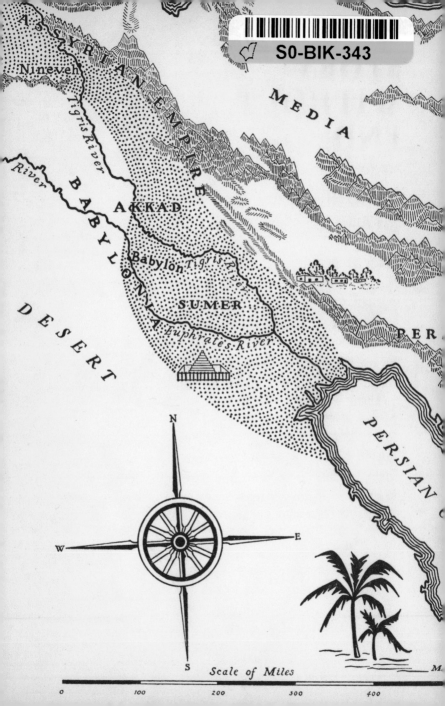

ASSYRIAN EMPIRE

Nineveh

MEDIA

Tigris River

River

BABYLONIA

AKKAD

Babylon

Tigris River

SUMER

Euphrates River

DESERT

PER

PERSIAN G

N

W   E

S

Scale of Miles

0   100   200   300   400

M

SO-BIK-343

CHAPTER ONE

The Rise of the Hebrew People

THERE is a stretch of land in the Near East covering Iraq, Syria, and Palestine that is of considerable importance today because it is a connecting link between the oil deposits of Western Asia and the Mediterranean Sea.

This same area was coveted also in ancient days, but not for the same reason. Some four thousand years ago nations fought for it because of the trade routes that crisscrossed it, for it was then the center of a busy world, connecting Egypt, Babylonia, and the Mediterranean Sea.

It was also the most fertile area of Western Asia, the "breadbasket" of the flourishing empires in the vicinity. A belt of fertility stretched through it, starting at the Persian Gulf and circling to the northwest, then gently branching in a southwesterly direction through Syria and Palestine to the borders of Egypt. The belt thus formed a semicircle and became known as the Fertile Crescent. To the south of the Crescent lay the vast Arabian desert, in which nomadic peoples perpetually moved about in search of precious food and water for themselves and their flocks.

Most of the peoples who inhabited the Fertile Crescent and the desert to the south four thousand years ago were SEMITES.* This is a modern term applied to the ancient Babylonians, Assyrians, Phoenicians, Moabites, Hebrews, and many others, whose languages were similar in roots, inflection, and sentence structure, and who, according to Biblical tradition, were descendants of Shem, the son of Noah. These Semitic peoples left their imprint on history; out of their conflicting ambitions and the interplay of their beliefs and customs came much of the civilization that later developed in the Western World.

The Hebrews of the Crescent, like the nomadic Semites of the desert, wandered about in family clans. The clan members considered themselves of the same blood and referred to their kinsmen as "brothers." To the nomads, the clan was a protection, their guarantee of a livelihood, especially when another clan threatened their food and water. The individual, therefore, gave his primary allegiance to the clan, and a strong sense of solidarity existed within the group.

All property of the members was owned in common, that is, it belonged to the clan as a whole. This included the tents they slept in, the clothes they wore, and the sheep and goats they tended. Each individual's well-being depended upon the welfare of the clan, and since they were "blood-brothers" all shared equally in the wealth and substance of the clan. There was such a strong sense of equality

---

* This term and others, set in small capitals on their first appearance, are explained in greater detail in the Glossary.

CONTENTS

To Lillian, and to the memory of Dorothy, devoted wives and rare companions, whose love and countless sacrifices made possible the writing of this book.

Copyright, 1949, by
Solomon Landman and Benjamin Efron

LIBERTY BOOK CLUB EDITION

199

DESIGNED BY MAURICE SERLE KAPLAN

PRINTED IN THE UNITED STATES OF AMERICA

Story Without End

AN INFORMAL HISTORY OF THE JEWISH PEOPLE

SOLOMON LANDMAN *and* BENJAMIN EFRON

HENRY HOLT AND COMPANY

NEW YORK

within the clan that not even the accepted head or leader could force others to do his bidding; he had to rely mainly on the good will of his kinsmen for obedience. It was a primitive sort of solidarity, infused with a democratic "each for all and all for each" psychology.

Sometimes a number of clans came together to form a tribe under an accepted leader, who today would be called a patriarch. The tribe was often only a temporary confederation, organized to pool the resources of the clans or jointly to protect their grazing lands against intruders. If, after a time, the area could no longer support the large numbers dwelling in it, the tribe would break up again into its constituent clans, each clan going its separate way.

The ancient Semitic tribes believed that everything in life and nature was controlled by gods, and that one particular god controlled the fate of each tribe. Each clan, as well as each family household within the clan, had its own god, to whom the members showed allegiance through various sacrifices and rituals. Although the clan god superseded the several household gods, the people generally performed the accustomed ceremonies to their household deities in order to insure themselves of whatever added protection those lesser gods could give.

It was truly a god-conscious and god-fearing age. The people believed in all sorts of deities—gods that controlled the rain, the rivers, lightning, thunder, epidemics, and every other manifestation of nature and life. It was of the utmost importance to the ancient Semites, therefore, to keep their gods friendly toward them, so that all would go well with the tribe, clan, or household.

Even though each clan or tribe had its own god, the

3

early peoples also respected the gods of the other tribes and feared to displease them. Thus, if a clan settled down in a land ruled by another god, they worshiped that god as the natives of the region did, while also continuing their allegiance to their own god. They believed that the gods actually lived in the land they ruled, had special powers over the forces of nature in that area, and that therefore, if the new settlers were to prosper, they had to seek the good will of the god of the land, too.

Their chief mode of worship was the sacrifice, a dramatic expression of the bond with their god. In desert civilization, this rite usually consisted of burning a carefully selected animal of the flock as an offering to the god, on an altar erected wherever the clan believed the god to live, followed by a solemn, sacred meal, in which all the kinsmen tasted the sacrifice. This was considered a form of communion with the deity. Sometimes, to make sure that the communion was properly established, the blood of the sacrifice was sprinkled on the altar and on the people.

The lives of the Semitic nomads were dominated by their primitive beliefs. They believed in magic, that is, that human beings could control such invisible powers as gods, spirits, demons, or the souls of material things. They believed they could employ these magic powers to protect themselves against harm by wearing amulets and charms, or to inflict punishment on others by uttering special curses or by rubbing blood on sacred stones. Many of their prohibitions and taboos were also based on their belief in magic, as, for instance, the taboo against the sacrifice of an animal and its young on the same day. They feared that in some mysterious way such activities could lead to the destruction of their whole flock. Their fears and beliefs thus led to a host of ceremonies, customs, and taboos which became part of their religion.

Many places became sacred to primitive peoples: rivers, trees, springs, mountains, and caves, wherever they believed gods or spirits dwelled; and here they built shrines for worship. Families, assigned a communal pasture for their grazing ground, usually revered the holy places and sacred springs in their area. The special ceremonies they performed there became part of the traditional rituals of the household, rituals the family continued to observe in addition to the ceremonials prescribed by the clan or tribe.

They observed other rituals besides the sacrifices. They performed various rites of purification, by which the people made themselves fit to come into the presence of the deity. On certain occasions the assembled tribe invoked aloud the name of the deity; sometimes there were shouts of praise, accompanied by ritual dances. Special ceremonies were performed during sacred seasons, such as sheep-shearing time in the desert or harvest time in the settled, agricultural areas, to make certain that the god would provide for them in abundance. The various rituals were executed with great care by priests who were specially set aside for that purpose; for the god, they believed, required the ceremonies to be performed with exactitude.

The clans of those days, then, were brotherhoods, bound closely to a god who was their protector. All they did, all that happened to them—whatever occurred, either in nature or in the fortunes of the individual or the tribe—was regarded as an act of the deity who was their lord and master. When a great monarch of that period, about four thousand years ago, Hammurabi of Babylonia, wrote about some irrigation work he had completed, he started his account with the words: "When Anu and Bel entrusted me with the rule of Sumer and Akkad . . ." Anu and Bel were the gods of those lands. Even the stone on which Hammurabi's famous code of laws is engraved depicts at the head of it the god of the land giving him the laws.

It was out of just such Semitic clans of the desert that the Hebrew patriarch, Abraham, organized a tribe. In belief and in mode of life his people were in the main indistinguishable from their Semitic neighbors of the desert. He gave them his own god, *El Shaddai* (God Almighty), as the god of the whole tribe.

Thus, some four thousand years ago, there was started a loose confederation of clans, which continued to call themselves after the names of their patriarchs or leaders, such as Israel, Benjamin, Joseph, and so forth. But they were given a new name, a collective name, when their nomadic wanderings brought them westward across the Euphrates River to Palestine (then known as Canaan), a name given to them by the Palestinian natives who referred to them as *Ivri-im* because they had come from *e-ver*, meaning "the other side" of the Euphrates. From this was derived the name by which they came to be known, "Hebrews."

Although, like other Semitic tribes in the desert, they started out in history as polytheists, that is, worshipers of many gods, it was the Hebrews alone who developed the idea of monotheism, the belief that there is only one God in the universe. It was the Hebrew deity, not the gods of the other Semitic tribes, who became the Universal God of Western civilization. The process by which the primitive

The Rise of the Hebrew People

religious ideas of the Hebrews were transformed makes one of the most significant chapters in world history, for the development of ETHICAL MONOTHEISM by the Hebrews was a very important contribution to world progress.

After a considerable period of wandering, Abraham's tribe of Hebrews settled in Palestine and continued their pastoral existence in that fertile region. Their wandering, however, did not cease altogether; for other nomads, also seeking a permanent abode in that land, forced some of the Hebrew clans and tribes to move elsewhere. Moreover, occasional droughts lessened the food supply, and consequently one or another of the Hebrew clans detached itself from the tribe to seek better or more secure pasture land. Sometimes the Hebrew clans disagreed among themselves, despite their allegiance to the same god; the Bible refers to a number of quarrels, between Abraham and Lot, Jacob and Esau, to mention only a few. At one time, as a result of serious drought in Palestine, a number of Hebrew clans wandered to the southwest and settled in territory on the easternmost border of Egypt, while the rest of the Hebrews remained in Palestine.

Joseph, one of the Hebrews who left Palestine in this migration, rose to high position in Egypt; in fact, he became second in authority to the Pharaoh, as the Egyptian monarchs were called. Through Joseph's influence, the Hebrew clans that had left Palestine were given permission to settle permanently in this border section east of the Nile Delta, a region referred to in the Bible as Goshen.

Their early years in Egypt were peaceful and fruitful, and in succeeding generations the Hebrews prospered and multiplied, but bad times hit them when the Hyksos and

7

other peoples to the north began to attack Egypt. To defend the country against the invaders, the Egyptian ruler ordered supply depots and fortifications built in the Goshen region. This called for large numbers of workers, which the Pharaoh got by pressing into service the Hebrews who were settled there. The Hebrews were thus reduced to slavery, to forced labor on the project.

Like all nomads, the Hebrews were proud and independent; they resented the loss of their freedom, but had to submit, for Egypt was a great power with a strong army. They began to feel friendless and unprotected; they believed, as did the other peoples of that time, that a vanquished people lost their god as well as their freedom. They felt that the god of Abraham had deserted them altogether.

At this critical time in the life of the Hebrews, Moses appeared on the scene. He was a man with an unshakable faith in "Jahweh," the name by which Moses referred to the god of Abraham; he made it his mission in life to free the Hebrews from slavery and to reunite them with Jahweh. But first he had to convince them that they still had a god of their own. In doing this he brought to the Hebrews a new understanding of the deity: their god was not a mere GOD-OF-THE-LAND attached to the land the tribe owned; Jahweh was their protector wherever they lived and they were Jahweh's people forever. This deep association of the Hebrews with Jahweh, which Moses impressed on his people in Egypt, later became one of the main tenets of the Hebrew faith.

Inspired by Moses' faith in the power of Jahweh, the dejected Hebrews began to lift up their heads, to look forward to their liberation, even though between them and freedom stood the formidable army of Pharaoh. But with such a man as Moses as their leader even miracles seemed possible, so they prepared for their escape under his guidance.

In the time of Moses, Egypt was subject to plagues, the annual overflow of the Nile River leaving mosquitoes and frequent epidemics in its wake. And since Egypt was a fertile land, it was subject to foreign invasions as well. Some Egyptian writers also referred to these as plagues. Moses chose a time when both types of plague were harassing Egypt to lead the Hebrews out of the country. The start of the revolt came so unexpectedly that Pharaoh was caught unaware. To head off the escaping Hebrews, however, Pharaoh sent his chariot army into action, and it caught up with them just as they were nearing the Red Sea. The Hebrews faltered for a moment when they came to the edge of the water, but assured by Moses that the tide was low enough to permit them to cross, in they went. They made their way to the opposite shore.

When the Egyptians came to the Red Sea, they, too, plunged ahead, but the heavy wheels of the chariots began to sink deeper and deeper into the muddy bottom; the horses reared and plunged but could make little headway. Nor could they turn around and get back to shore, for behind them were more chariots, more horses, more Egyptians yelling and tugging, sinking deeper into the mud.

The Hebrews, safe on the other side, looked back and beheld the flower of the Egyptian army drowning in the water; they felt that their deliverance was nothing short of a miracle, a sign of the great power of Jahweh, about which Moses had talked so glowingly and so confidently. With a

deep sense of gratitude they accepted Moses as the spokesman of Jahweh and their leader.

When the Hebrews once again took up their lives in
the South-Palestine desert as free and independent tribes,
Moses set about his appointed task of creating one people
out of the liberated tribes, a people dedicated to Jahweh,
the author of their liberty. He weaned them from the rituals
they had adopted during the generations they had spent
living in the midst of foreign peoples, in the days when
they believed their god had deserted them. He created new
ways of life and worship for all the clans to observe, a
national religion based on the recognition of Jahweh as the
one god for all the Hebrews. He made them feel that they
were more than members of individual clans claiming a
common descent, that they were in reality a closely knit
people, bound together by their common worship of Jahweh.

There were other Semitic peoples in the time of Moses,
about thirty-three or thirty-four hundred years ago, who
had also confederated around a tribal god. But it was the
genius of Moses to make the Hebrews feel much closer to
their god, more intimately and intensely associated with
him. It was this emphasis upon the special connection of
the Hebrews with Jahweh that, more than anything else,
laid the ground for the future religious development of the
Hebrews.

During the forty years Moses spent in the desert with
his people, he impressed upon them that a special pact, a
binding agreement called the Covenant, existed between
them and Jahweh. This covenant assured Jahweh's people, the Hebrews, his love and protection in return for

their performance of the prescribed sacrifices, rituals, and ceremonials. It also decreed the principles, morals, and ethics that the Hebrews were to observe in their conduct toward one another.

The commandments of the covenant became sacred to the Hebrews because Moses, the accepted spokesman of Jahweh, personally heard and judged all disputes that came up between the people. He based his decisions on the rules of the covenant and thus established them as the principles of justice they, the children of Jahweh, were to follow.

All nomadic tribes regarded themselves as families, and considered the security of the individual as one of their main objectives. But Moses made this way of life a sacred part of the covenant between his people and Jahweh; he made it an obligation for Hebrews to treat one another with consideration and in a spirit of equality. He instilled in them a deep-seated faith in Jahweh as a god who was concerned about the way they lived with one another.

From Moses they learned to believe that there was none like him among the *elim*—the Hebrew word for the "gods" —either in power or in justice. They also believed that Jahweh demanded complete identification with him alone in return for his protection and interest. Thus, under the influence of Moses, the ISRAELITES developed a deep and intimate attachment to Jahweh, a closer unity among themselves, and a strong national feeling based on the covenant with their god.

CHAPTER TWO

The Development of the Hebrew Nation

A NATIONAL consciousness is not sufficient in itself to give a people a feeling of stability. What the liberated Hebrews needed to give them a sense of permanence was a land which they could call their own and which, at the same time, could produce enough to satisfy their needs. That land was Palestine, where, as Moses knew, a number of Hebrew tribes had settled a long time before.

But Moses did not himself lead the Israelites into Palestine; he had become old by the time he had finished his work of uniting the tribes and died before he could completely realize his dream. His chief lieutenant, Joshua, led them into the land to join the other Hebrews.

The native Hebrew tribes were settled in different parts of Palestine, not in a continuous stretch of territory. The Hebrews who came out of the desert could not settle in a single area either, for other Palestinian peoples were occupying the sections between the various Hebrew settlements.

After many years, during which a number of small wars were fought, the Hebrews were finally able to establish themselves in a few sections of Palestine. Some remained in the south, while a larger number settled in the central highlands in the north.

As the Hebrew tribes of the north increased in population they spread out to the west and to the south of the highlands. This disturbed a number of Amorite tribes nearby, who feared the growing might of the Hebrews. Under a great general, Sisera, a large Amorite army gathered for an attack upon the Hebrews. Faced by a powerful array of infantry and chariots, the highlanders called upon their fellow Hebrews for assistance.

The call for aid was sent out by Deborah, a woman who was a judge among the Hebrews of the central highlands. The judges of those days were leaders whom the tribesmen consulted as their forefathers had done in the time of Moses, when some problem arose.

Whether it was a dispute between individuals or a matter concerning a whole clan or tribe, the judge, of course, was expected to render his decision on the basis of *mishpat*—the Hebrew word which refers to the ideas of justice which Moses had developed in the desert. The judge was the keeper or guardian of *mishpat*, justice; and as such, was highly respected.

Deborah's request for aid was answered by some of the Hebrew clans who occupied land in and near the contested area, and she selected a man by the name of Barak to lead the Hebrew army. The Hebrews engaged the Amorites on the plains of Esdraelon in the northern highlands, and after a furious battle in a thunderstorm the Amorites were defeated. It must have been a truly great victory, for Hebrew poets made song-stories of the event, glorifying Jahweh for his triumph over the Palestinian *Baal*, by which name the Hebrews referred to the gods of that country. The "Song of Deborah," one of these poems, transmitted from generation to generation by Hebrew singers, is one of the oldest pieces of ancient Hebrew literature that has come down to us; it is included in the fifth chapter of the Book of Judges, in the Old Testament.

After this decisive victory, the Hebrew army disbanded, the soldiers returning to their respective homes. But again and again the Hebrew tribes of the central highlands had to pool their manpower to ward off attackers, for they were situated in a coveted and strategic area of Palestine, right in the path of nomadic tribes who from time to time came out of the desert to invade Palestine in search of a permanent home. Each victory over the marauding tribes gave the Hebrews a greater claim to the land they occupied, and in fact, won for them the friendship of the nearby non-Hebrew tribes, who came to look upon them as the military defenders of the eastern borders of Palestine.

The growing power of the Hebrews attracted the attention of the Philistines, a highly developed people who lived on the western coast of Palestine, along the Mediterranean Sea. The Philistines, from whom the name Palestine was derived, were ruled by merchants and traders who controlled the trade routes that connected the country with Egypt and Babylonia. These trade routes yielded a rich harvest in tolls levied on the caravans that made their way across Palestine. But they had to pass through the region of the central plains, and to the north and south of these plains were Hebrew tribes.

The Philistines saw in the Hebrews a threat to their supremacy in the land. They feared that once the Hebrews gained control of these trade routes, the source of their wealth would be cut off and their power in the country would come to an end.

The Philistines, therefore, attacked the Hebrews, overcame some of the scattered villages and placed garrisons of troops among them to keep them in check, while the Philistine armored chariots rode on further east. A hastily organized Hebrew army tried to stop them in the plains of Esdraelon but met a crushing defeat. As a result, a number of Hebrew tribes were forced to pay tribute to their conquerors.

The national spirit of the highland Hebrews was aroused, now that some of the tribes had lost their independence. They resented being under the yoke of a foreign god; they resented also having to pay tribute to live on the very land they had defended with their blood from the time of Deborah.

Meanwhile, in Gilead, on the eastern border of Palestine close to the Arabian desert, beyond the conquests of the Philistines, other Hebrew tribes were facing danger from another quarter. A warlike people, the Ammonites, were coming up out of the desert, hacking their way into Palestine. The frightened Hebrews in their path rallied to the defense of their homeland. Led by Saul, a member of the clan of Kish, of the tribe of Benjamin, they drove the Ammonites back to the desert.

The elders of the Hebrew tribes now decided that they

could no longer afford to disperse the army as they had done before, after each successful defense against invaders. They met at Gilgal, in northern Palestine, in the year 1028 B.C. and organized themselves into the kingdom of Israel, selecting Saul as their first king. Thereupon, Saul and his son, Jonathan, led the army of Israel against the Philistines and drove them out of the country, but only temporarily.

The kingdom of Israel, over which Saul ruled, comprised only the northern Hebrew tribes. The southern tribes continued to live independently, for the territory these tribes inhabited was situated off the coveted trade routes, so that they had not been harassed by the Philistines and had not felt the need for union with the other tribes. The federated tribes of Israel, therefore, represented only the first step toward the merging of all the tribes into a single Hebrew nation, the ultimate aim that Moses had set for Jahweh's people.

Though the southernmost tribes were not part of the kingdom of Israel, a southerner by the name of David did become one of the leading officers of Saul's army. Saul early recognized David's military ability; he made him a general and gave him one of his daughters in marriage. Legend has it that David's popularity had grown with his defeat of Goliath, the Philistine strongman and champion. It increased as he won battle after battle.

The popularity David enjoyed did not please Saul, for he began to suspect that David had his eyes upon the throne. Saul also knew that if David ever seized the throne, he would put Saul and his family to death, as was the custom in those days. Saul, therefore, planned to do away with

David; but his own son, Jonathan, a warm friend of David's, warned him to leave the court and go into hiding.

David fled, taking with him his small band of devoted followers. He became a freebooter, hiring himself out to any king or landowner who would pay him to protect his property. In the course of these activities, he was employed by Achish, a Philistine king, which to Saul was a traitorous act, for the Philistines were archenemies of the Hebrews of Israel, even though they were not then at war.

As a matter of fact, the Philistines were actually preparing all-out war against Saul, to establish their supremacy in Palestine once and for all. But just before they attacked, they ordered David and his men to a Philistine city to get them out of the way; for David was, after all, a Hebrew, and they feared that in the heat of battle he might decide to come to the aid of Israel and Jahweh.

It was a fateful war, which ended with the utter defeat of Israel at Mount Gilboa, and the death of Saul. By this defeat, Israel lost its independence, and was reduced to a vassal state of the Philistines.

After the death of Saul, David returned to the southern area where the independent Hebrew tribes lived, and there for a number of years he worked to organize them into a nation. He also persuaded some of the non-Hebrew tribes in the region to consolidate with the Hebrews for mutual protection against the Philistines, who were planning to overrun all of Palestine. David's efforts were successful, and the elders of the tribes met and elected him as their king. The southern country they thus formed was called Judah. Its capital city was Hebron.

David's main ambition was to unite all of the Hebrews,

both the southern and northern tribes, under his kingship. Although the tribes of Israel did not like the idea of being ruled by a southerner, the elders of Israel, remembering his skill as a fighter, felt that in David lay their only hope for freedom. So in 1016 B.C., the elders journeyed to David's capital city, and there, in the name of Jahweh, anointed him king of Israel. Now, at last, all the Hebrew tribes were united under one ruler.

David realized that his throne would never be completely secure unless the Philistines were overcome, but before he could fight the Philistines successfully, he knew he must bring the rival tribes of Judah and Israel closer together. Hebron could no longer serve as a capital; besides being an unfortified city, it was completely Judahite, which, he feared, might alienate the northern tribes. David therefore looked about for a new capital on neutral ground, neither southern nor northern.

There was just such a city in the mountainous district between Israel and Judah, the city of Jerusalem, inhabited by the Jebusites, a non-Hebrew people. Besides being a good fortress, it had value as a commercial center, for the main trade routes passed right through it.

David attacked the city and captured it. He then established it as his capital, permitting the Jebusites to remain in it as his subjects, which meant that the Jebusites accepted Jahweh as their god and became part of the Hebrew nation.

The Philistines, recognizing the danger of David's growing power, assembled their forces to put him down. But David met them and destroyed their army so completely that they were helpless ever again to threaten his kingdom.

The Hebrews were now completely free; their god had conquered their enemies, and David's power in Palestine was established.

David built a palace on Mount Zion, one of the hills of Jerusalem. He triumphantly brought to Jerusalem the sacred Ark of the Covenant, in which were kept the commandments of Jahweh, and erected for it a temporary shrine. It became the symbol of the unity of the Hebrews around Jahweh and implied that Jerusalem was his abode. This shrine also became the center of Hebrew worship, overshadowing the local altars and shrines at which the people were accustomed to worship Jahweh. In this way, David elevated Jahweh to the position of a truly national god. He made Jerusalem the religious, as well as the political, capital of the united Hebrew nation.

Under David, the Hebrews became the dominant power in Palestine. He conquered the Edomites and Moabites, Semitic peoples of Palestine related to the Hebrews, who lived to the east of Judah; he also subdued the Syrians of Damascus, making them all pay him tribute as their over-lord. Through these victories David became a "king of kings," and Jahweh a "god of gods." Even non-Hebrew tribes that lived within the borders of the Hebrew kingdom recognized Jahweh as a conquering god, and true to the god-of-the-land belief of the time, many of them adopted Jahweh as their own god. All in all, David brought to the Hebrews a sense of strength and security they had never before enjoyed.

While all the Hebrews now seemed united, actually all was not well in the land. Beneath the surface the hostility between the northern and southern sections still smoldered.

In fact, it increased. For David took away from the elders of the tribes their time-honored right to decide appeals in cases where Hebrews felt the decision of the judges had been incorrect, by decreeing that all appeals must be made to him, personally, at Jerusalem. This not only lowered the prestige of the elders; it represented a clean break with the tribal customs of the past. But David was more interested in strengthening his own power in the land than in honoring established customs. The king was the law, just as was the case in the other despotisms of the time.

David's wars, furthermore, aggravated the discontent in the country, for even in those days wars cost money. To obtain the funds, he levied heavy taxes and sent special collectors to see that the people paid them. The royal household which had to be maintained in peace and war was an expensive item, also; the taxes were therefore perpetually high.

The taxes fell most heavily upon the poorer landowners. Some land simply did not yield very much, and to meet the taxes the poorer landowners had to go to their more fortunate kinsmen to borrow money. In some sections of Israel, where things were done on a business basis, the wealthier Hebrews charged interest, and made the small landowners mortgage their farms to secure the loan. When they couldn't repay, the mortgages were foreclosed, the farms were taken by the creditors, and the dispossessed families either migrated to the cities or hired themselves out to the new owners as tenants or sharecroppers. Sometimes, Hebrew families were enslaved altogether to work off a debt they had contracted.

In David's reign many Israelite families began to feel the

pinch of debts and found themselves confronted with the
loss of their farms, and consequently, their freedom. In
Judah, in the south, which was more pastoral, the people
were not so hard-pressed. It was among the poorer landowners of Israel, therefore, that David's popularity began
to wane. In fact, the people of Israel actually revolted once,
under the leadership of David's own son, Absalom, who
tried to capitalize on the discontent of the people to seize
the throne from his father. David's army made short shrift
of the rebellion, and Absalom and many others were killed.

It is interesting to note that in later times, when the
Hebrews no longer had an independent country, they
looked back upon David with yearning, as the king who
had brought glory to the nation. His faults were forgotten, and the House of David, as the royal family he started
is known, became sacred to the Hebrews. In the case of
David things did not work out as Shakespeare stated in his
play, *Julius Caesar:* "The evil that men do lives after them,
the good is oft interred with their bones."

David ruled a long time and when he died, his son,
Solomon, came to the throne. Solomon had grown up in
a royal household, the son of a king. He had developed a
set of values and an outlook on life different from that of
the average Hebrew. He had had greater contact with the
world outside, had traveled, and been impressed with the
wealth and splendor of the oriental cities and countries he
had seen. He, too, wanted to be a great king, a potentate
ruling amid magnificent surroundings, which to him were
signs of greatness. His capital city must be second to none;
but compared to the royal cities of Egypt and Phoenicia,
Jerusalem was a country town.

He therefore decided to create the splendor he valued so highly. He built in Jerusalem a wonderful Temple for Jahweh, made of carefully selected stone and lined with cedarwood covered with gold. He erected a magnificent palace to house his many wives, and a special one for the Egyptian princess he had married. He put up a very expensive building for the reception of ambassadors from other lands, and each building was ornamented with gold, precious stones, and ivory. He had special stones brought in to pave the streets of Jerusalem, and dressed his servants and attendants in striking uniforms.

The city must surely have been a dazzling sight for the work-a-day Hebrews who came from farms and villages to make their sacrifices at the Temple in Jerusalem at festival time. They must have gaped, the way visitors still do today when they see the skyscrapers of New York for the first time. Solomon must have impressed them as a man of extraordinary ability and wisdom. His fame spread beyond the borders of his own kingdom, for even the Queen of Sheba came from her distant Ethiopia to view for herself the marvels of Jerusalem.

But somebody had to pay for all this magnificence. Most of the materials used in the buildings had to be brought from distant lands, a very costly undertaking in those days of hand labor. Solomon had to use thousands of skilled craftsmen, besides some hundred and seventy-five thousand unskilled laborers. Where did the money and labor come from?

Like the Pharaoh who had enslaved the Hebrews of Goshen before the time of Moses, Solomon reduced to forced labor various Palestinian tribes, and also ordered thousands of Hebrews to give him labor service for four months of the year without pay. He contracted with Hiram, king of Tyre, the capital of Phoenicia, to supply him for a stipulated sum the skilled artisans and special materials he needed.

Part of the money came from the tributes sent in by the nations David had conquered, and some he derived from tolls levied on the caravans that passed through his land, for Solomon had cleared the area around Jerusalem of desert bandits and had made the city a great center of trade. Still another source of income was the profit from his own business, for Solomon himself had become a great trader, sending many caravans and ships to distant parts of the world.

Money was coming in, yes, but not enough; for Solomon's needs were great. Just to feed his harem and royal household for one day his agents had to deliver to him, as the Bible tells us, "thirteen measures of fine flour; threescore measures of meal, ten fat oxen, twenty oxen out of the pastures; a hundred sheep, besides harts, roebucks, fallow deer and fatted fowl."

To procure additional revenue Solomon levied still heavier taxes throughout the country, appointing special tax collectors for each district. In laying out these tax districts he disregarded tribal lines in the interest of efficient collections. The tribes of the north chafed at this contempt for their group identity and looked upon his arbitrary districting as an attack upon their tribal independence within the kingdom.

It was the people who paid for the magnificence Solomon prized, and they did not like it, particularly in Israel where the great majority of the Hebrews lived. They had not cared for David's reign; but the burdens put upon them by his son were quite intolerable. In fact, from Solomon's reign on, the number of landless and enslaved Hebrews grew larger; and the wealth of the landed aristocrats increased.

One of the officials Solomon had appointed "over the burdens of Israel," Jeroboam ben Nebat, was induced by the leaders of the north to head a revolt, for Jeroboam was himself an Israelite. But before the revolt actually got under way, Solomon learned of it and sent a police force to arrest Jeroboam who fled to Egypt where the Pharaoh gave him refuge. The revolt, thus left leaderless, subsided; and Solomon ruled until he died.

Despite the hardships the people suffered, Solomon's reign did accomplish certain good things. He beautified the country with his palaces and gardens. He made Jerusalem a cosmopolitan city; brought the Hebrews into closer touch with the outside world through his fostering of trade; and opened up new occupations to the people by making Jerusalem an important center of commerce. But along with all this, the people had to endure a tyrant, an oriental despot, typical of the other rulers of the time. And yet, perhaps because of the accomplishments of his reign, people attributed to Solomon great powers of wisdom, and his fame as a sage grew as generation after generation retold the ancient legends of his time.

When Solomon died, his son Rehoboam succeeded him to the throne. Judah had no quarrel with that, for the House of David was their royal line. But the Israelites did not recognize any hereditary royal line. The elders of the tribes had selected Saul as king, the elders had also proclaimed David king, and they felt that it was their right now to decide who should be the new king. They prized it as a sign of their independence, this right to select their king.

They wanted at this time, especially, to have a say in the matter, for Solomon had made life quite difficult for them. Rehoboam did not acknowledge Israel's right to make a decision in the matter of succession to the throne, so he decided to go up to Israel for the formal ceremony of coronation, to show the Israelites that he was their master. But he underestimated the Israelite spirit of independence. Before they would recognize him as their king, they demanded that he agree to certain conditions, that he lighten the load Solomon had placed upon them.

Rehoboam, brought up in the household of a potentate, resented his subjects' presuming to dictate to him. The kingship and all its privileges were rightfully his, simply as a descendant of the House of David. And so he said to the elders, "My father made your yoke heavy, and I will add to your yoke. My father chastised you with whips, but I will chastise you with scorpions!" Then he ordered his agent, Adoniram, to make his levy of forced labor.

The Israelites rose up in anger and stoned Adoniram to death. Rehoboam fled south to Jerusalem. The Israelites then recalled Jeroboam from Egypt and made him king over Israel. In this dramatic manner the Hebrews of Israel seceded from the united Hebrew kingdom David had established and became an independent country.

Thus, by 930 B.C., there were two Hebrew states again—

Judah in the south, under Rehoboam, with its capital in Jerusalem; and Israel in the central highlands to the north, under Jeroboam, with its capital in the unfortified town of Tirzah. Jahweh was still the god of both nations, but aside from this, there was no other bond between them.

CHAPTER THREE

Elijah, Champion of the Covenant

THE period of the two kingdoms was marked by the struggles of the kings of both Judah and Israel to maintain their independence. They were almost continually under attack either by the empire-hungry Assyrians and Babylonians to the northeast, or by Egypt to the southwest.

Palestine, with its important position on the Mediterranean and its profitable trade routes in the interior, became the battleground of empire. Like locusts, only much more destructively, the soldiers of the various conquerors descended upon the land and despoiled it. The Hebrew kings were forced to pay tribute at one time or another to Assyria, to Egypt, or to Babylonia. Sometimes they were left in peace, when the conquerors were busy elsewhere, but most often the kings of Judah and Israel had a difficult time keeping their thrones.

The people had a difficult time of it, too. Constant war, or preparation for war, kept the taxes high, while the tributes to foreign powers forced the kings to levy extra burdens upon the people in order to meet the payments exacted by the conquerors. To an increasing degree large numbers of independent Hebrew farmers became landless, their farms being taken from them for debts.

The growth of a landed aristocracy and a large class of landless peasants and slaves among the Hebrews was a development of tremendous significance in the history of the people. It represented a decided change in the Hebrew pattern of equality and consideration for one another that Moses had established as the Hebrew way of life, a pattern that was accepted as part of the covenant with Jahweh.

While they lived in the desert with Moses, the Hebrews had observed the covenant in their everyday life. The fact that they were then a pastoral people living in tribes made it easier to apply the covenant, for the tribe owned all the property the members used and the tribal leaders divided the products of the flocks among the kinsmen in the spirit of mutual responsibility and mutual aid. But when the Hebrews settled in Palestine, they came in contact with a different way of life. Palestine was a settled country. The people who occupied the western coastal region, on the Mediterranean, supported themselves largely through fishing, while the interior of the country was predominantly agricultural. True enough, there were shepherds in Palestine; but they were not nomads. In the pastoral regions, in the southern and northern highlands, the natives tended their flocks season after season in the same pasture lands. And for the first time in their experience, the Hebrews encountered city dwellers, who made their living in commerce, and who followed trades as craftsmen, and worked in other occupations as laborers.

The Hebrews now had to organize their communities along different lines. They had to settle on whatever land was available to them, wherever they could find it. No longer did a whole clan occupy all its territory in common. Instead, the land was divided into pasture fields and farms, and each family was given, by lot, its portion of the tribal property. But the parcel of land was not allotted to an individual. The family owned it, and it was understood that the land was to remain in the family's possession forever. In this way, the tribe insured the independence and livelihood of its members, for without land the alternative for a family was sharecropping or slavery. So it was considered as part of the sacred covenant for the land to be inalienable, that is, to be possessed forever by the family to which it had originally been allotted.

The Palestinians, on the other hand, were a commercially-minded people who treated land as real estate to be bought and sold like any other kind of merchandise. Although they also believed themselves to be bound to their gods by a pact, their covenant did not include the idea that a family had a sacred and inalienable right to its land.

The Hebrews, after many generations of living in Palestine, began to imitate the customs of their neighbors. They planted their fields the way the Palestinians did. This meant more than merely copying their method of plowing, seeding, tending, and harvesting. It included copying ancient Palestinian religious practices as well; for nothing, to the ancients, could succeed without the help of the god of the land, whose prescribed rituals had to be observed.

Like the Palestinians, the Hebrews made sacrifices of grains and fruits at planting and harvest times and at the start of the rainy season. They also held sacred processions, danced ritual dances, and performed many other of the rites of the Palestinian gods of the land. They, too, sacrificed grapes, in the form of wine, drinking the sacrifice like the Palestinians, and getting just as drunk.

Bit by bit, they adopted many other Palestinian customs, including the custom of taking possession of a kinsman's land, either by purchase or foreclosure. By the time of King David and King Solomon, this process of alienating land from the families who had inherited it had become a common practice among the Hebrews, and in the period of the divided kingdoms it became even more widespread.

The ancient idea that land must remain in the possession of the family that had originally received the grant did not die out altogether in Israel. There were some people who still held the custom sacred, although four or five hundred years had elapsed since the Hebrews had first settled in Palestine, as King Ahab, who ruled Israel about the middle of the ninth century B.C., found out. He tried to buy a vineyard near his palace grounds, but its owner Naboth refused to sell, claiming that it was a commandment of Jahweh that land must not be alienated from its hereditary owners.

King Ahab was angry, but he recognized Naboth's right to the land. When he told his queen, Jezebel, about his failure to purchase the vineyard, she was puzzled. The covenant with Jahweh was alien to her, since she was a foreigner, the daughter of the Phoenician king of Tyre, where there was no tradition against the sale of land. She wanted her husband to own the vineyard, so she forged Ahab's name to a letter accusing Naboth of blasphemy, and procured two witnesses to swear falsely against him at the trial, which was enough to have him condemned to death. She then told Ahab what she had done, but since he also desired the vineyard he permitted the frame-up to go through. Naboth and his whole family were executed, and according to the custom of the time in such cases, there being no heirs, the land automatically became the king's.

The Hebrews in the rural communities, when they heard of this injustice, were incensed at the criminal violation of the covenant. They were removed from the commercial centers of Palestine and had retained much of the old tribal life based on the traditional Hebrew customs that had been developed in the desert. The covenant was therefore sacred to them.

There was such indignation in the village of Gilead, in the countryside to the east beyond the Jordan River, that Elijah, a religious leader of the area, left Gilead and journeyed to the heart of Israel to arouse the peasants of the kingdom against Ahab. He denounced the king as a murderer and inveighed against him for becoming a party to Jezebel's contemptuous violation of Hebrew tradition. He condemned Ahab for taking possession of Naboth's vineyard and depriving him of his rights and his family of their inheritance. For no matter how lowly, said Elijah, every Hebrew had rights that no king could override.

The Hebrews were all children of Jahweh; they all enjoyed the rights guaranteed them in the covenant, and no person, even the king, could deprive them of those rights. Elijah's bold statement was extremely important, not merely because he was publicly berating a king in the days when kings were absolute monarchs; what made it significant was his insistence that there was a moral law that stood above the king, that kings and commoners alike were bound by its rules.

Elijah believed that all the greed and immorality that had crept into Hebrew life had come about because the people of the covenant were worshiping Palestinian Baals and had adopted too much of Palestinian customs and civilization. The alienation of land, the mortgaging of farms for loans, and the charging of interest to impoverished Hebrews were all prohibited by Jahweh in the covenant; those who did such things, said Elijah, were no longer Jahweh's people, but Baal's.

He warned the people that they must rid Hebrew life of all evidence of BAAL WORSHIP, if the covenant with Jahweh was to be kept.

He was the first Hebrew to proclaim that social justice, in the eyes of Jahweh, was more important than the rituals and sacrifices people performed. His was the first revolt that had as an aim the reinstituting of the covenant of the desert as the main religious belief of the Hebrews.

One of the disciples of Elijah, a man by the name of Elisha, following the instructions of Elijah, prevailed upon a military commander, Jehu, to lead a revolt against King Joram, Ahab's son, who had succeeded to the throne of Israel. Jehu was successful and established himself as the king, after which he destroyed all the shrines, images, and priests of Baal in the land of Israel. Then he settled down to rule, but in the same manner as the preceding kings: as a potentate, not as the administrator of *mishpat* (justice), the principle that Elijah had proclaimed as the essence of Hebrew existence.

King Jehu rooted out the symbols of Baal, but the spirit of Baalism remained, for the commercial economy of Palestine continued to dominate Hebrew life. The great merchants and landowners continued to run their businesses in the accustomed manner, for their own personal gain; and Jehu and his successors continued to run the state for the greater glory and power of their thrones.

A number of Hebrews, however, did make an attempt to recapture the spirit of the covenant as it had existed in the days of the desert. These people organized themselves into a sort of religious brotherhood under the leadership of Jonadab ben Rechab, gave up farming, renounced private property, and forbade wine drinking. The Rechabites, as they were called, were, however, but a tiny island in an ocean of agriculture, private property, and trade.

Theirs was not a real solution to the inequality and slavery that had developed among the Hebrews. They advocated a return to the "good old days" of nomadic tribal life. But the people were not content to give up their land and property and return to the primitive conditions of the Hebrew past, because they had become accustomed to the higher standard of living and civilization of Palestine. Yet the fact that some Hebrews became Rechabites shows how deeply people had been affected by Elijah's insistence that social justice and morality must be observed by all Hebrews as a sign of their devotion to Jahweh.

CHAPTER FOUR

The Prophets and the Struggle for Social Justice

MOST of the Hebrews, however, showed their devotion to Jahweh through the accustomed rituals and sacrifices at their temples and shrines. In spite of the wars, the people of Israel did have periods of prosperity to be thankful for, especially during the reign of Jeroboam II, 785 to 745 B.C., some years after Elijah's time. Assyria was then being attacked by the Babylonians, and since Egypt was occupied with its own problems, Jeroboam seized the opportunity to reconquer some of the territory Israel had lost, and even to expand his kingdom. Tributes of money and goods began to flow into the country from the vanquished peoples.

In imitation of the surrounding oriental kingdoms, Israel's men of wealth gave themselves to luxurious living. They built winter and summer palaces of hewn stone, and paneled them with ivory; they held lavish parties, feasting and drinking amid delicate perfumes and strains of music. Men and women alike sought the pleasures of carefree living. A contemporary visitor to Samaria, the capital of Israel, could easily have gained the impression that Israel was a happy and prosperous country.

But to one visitor, the PROPHET Amos, it was nothing of the kind. In fact, when he journeyed to the cities of Israel to sell his wool and other produce, his heart burned with wrath. He was a hard-working shepherd from the village of Tekoah, a semiarid region in the rural section of Judah, where a man had to struggle hard against nature to make a living. The extravagance of the aristocracy was nothing short of sinful, wicked waste to Amos.

There was too great inequality of wealth in Israel, too many ragged, underfed children, too many slumlike dwellings. He was distressed by the large number of Hebrew slaves and sharecroppers he saw, people who had once been independent farmers owning their own land. It was the wealth which these oppressed Hebrews were producing that the rich were squandering.

To Amos, the immoral behavior of the ruling classes and the enslavement of the poorer Hebrews were serious violations of the sacred covenant with Jahweh. He came from a section of Judah where the Hebrews were wont to help one another rather than profit from a neighbor's temporary difficulties; in his community, the simple *mishpat* of early Hebrew pastoral life still obtained. But in Israel the poor man had no place to go for help or justice. In ancient days judges of the tribes, like Deborah, had administered justice according to the covenant. But the judges of Israel in the time of Jeroboam II were using their positions to feather their own nests. They demanded bribes before they made decisions; and since the wealthy alone could afford to pay them, most of the cases were settled in favor of the rich and powerful.

Filled with disgust and anger at all he had seen, Amos stood one day near the temple at Beth-El, in Israel, in the year 760 B.C., watching the throngs make holiday, for it was a special day of celebration in honor of one of Jeroboam's victories. Well-dressed Israelites were bringing fat cattle and beautiful doves for sacrifices at the altar. Their self-satisfied smiles as they left the temple pained Amos. To him it seemed they were saying, "Surely Jahweh must be pleased with me for the fine sacrifice I brought."

A feeling of revulsion seized Amos. In his mind's eye he saw again the ragged children and wretched hovels of the poor, and the slaves toiling in the hot sun. How could Jahweh be pleased with any of these people, who permitted, and even caused, such miserable conditions in the country?

Suddenly, in the midst of all the laughter and gaiety, he found himself speaking to the crowd in a thundering voice. Fools! What fools to rejoice over the destruction of their enemies! Didn't they know that they themselves were headed for destruction? What else could be their fate, since they "sell the righteous for silver, and the needy for a pair of shoes . . . and store up violence and robbery in their palaces?" All that they valued, all their wealth was derived from enslaving the poor, from business so crooked it amounted to robbery, and from the spoils of war.

The nation of Israel deserved no other end than destruction, Amos continued. It was against the will of Jahweh to permit such suffering and injustice. Nor would it help to "bring your sacrifices in the morning and your tithes after three days, and offer a sacrifice of thanksgiving." No ritual or ceremony could atone for their wickedness, for Jahweh was not interested in such things. "Seek good and not evil . . . and establish justice" in the land—that is what Jahweh wished.

The Hebrews listened, startled. How could he say Jahweh was angry with them? Hadn't they won many battles and wasn't the country more prosperous than it had ever been? Wasn't that proof enough that Jahweh was in their midst? What nonsense was this man talking?

They didn't know Jahweh at all, said Amos, else they would understand. The Hebrews were not Jahweh's favorites. The Philistines, the Kushites, all peoples were Jahweh's, no less than the Hebrews. Jahweh expected *all* humanity to live justly, not just the Hebrews. And if they lived in evil ways—if they were not just in their dealings with one another—then He would be against them, Hebrews or not. Especially would He be angry with the Hebrews, for with them had He made a covenant.

Only justice in the government, and in the relations between every person and his neighbor, could please God. "Let justice flow like water, and righteousness like a perennial stream." Otherwise, the Hebrews would lose their nation, king, and everything else.

The aristocracy and the priests were disturbed lest Amos arouse a spirit of rebellion in the land, so they ordered him to go back where he came from, to Judah. But he continued to preach his ideas of God and religion, and there were people who dared to listen, who recorded and cherished his words and ideas.

About twenty years later, when Jeroboam II died, the

kingdom of Israel entered a period of unrest, a period during which the country was menaced by the conquering armies of Egypt and Assyria. In those days, in the 740's B.C., another Prophet, an Israelite by the name of Hosea, rose up to preach against the injustice and inequality in the land.

Like Elijah, he opposed Baal worship, for with Baal worship had come the Palestinian practice of private ownership of land, cattle, and slaves; with it had come the concentration of wealth in the hands of a few, and the resulting impoverishment of the Hebrew peasantry. Only when the people of Israel would acknowledge Jahweh and the covenant, when they would operate their farms and businesses according to Hebrew *mishpat*, only then would their hardships be relieved, said Hosea.

He was saddened by the belief of the Hebrews that God lived in the shrines upon the sacred hills, concerned only with answering their requests for wealth and good crops and victories of all kinds, favors that would be granted them because of the splendid sacrifices they brought to the temple. No, said he, God lives in the hearts of the people; to have God with you it was necessary to treat people with love as well as with justice.

They were a wayward people, the Hebrews, said Hosea. They were like his own wife, Gomer, who had once been beautiful and, seemingly, happy. But one day she had left him to lead a life of sin, and for years he had heard nothing of her. And then one day, he saw a decrepit-looking woman being sold in the market place as a slave. With a heart full of pity he came close to look at the unfortunate creature. It was his wife! His heart was grieved at the sight of her. He outbid the others and brought her home, to restore her to her former beautiful self through his love and kindness. So would it be with Israel! Though they had strayed from the right path, God would not forsake them.

Even if the nation was taken into captivity, said Hosea, it would not matter. Therefore it was futile to make an alliance with Egypt against Assyria, or with Assyria against Egypt. That was not Israel's main problem, nor was it the road to real prosperity; what Israel needed was to be restored to the good graces of God. But truly to worship God, Hosea told the Israelites, they must love their fellow men and regard them as brothers, as the ancient Hebrews used to look upon their kinsmen. His stress on love as the standard of human conduct was a new idea in those days; it was the first time anyone had mentioned it as an essential of religion. It was certainly not the kind of feeling the wealthy Hebrews were showing toward the Hebrews they enslaved.

Neither Amos nor Hosea was able to change the ideas of the Hebrews, nor the course of events. The kings continued their intrigues with the powerful rulers that surrounded them; the common people continued to suffer oppression; the mode of worship of the Hebrews continued as before, emphasizing primitive rituals and sacrifices, not a person's conduct toward his fellow man, as the chief expression of their bond with Jahweh. But Amos and Hosea did have disciples, men who took their teachings to heart and who spread their ideas gradually among the people.

Nor did the voices of protest cease. From the year 740 B.C. and for many years afterwards, another Prophet, Isaiah, spoke up in the name of Jahweh. Although himself a nobleman and an adviser to kings, Isaiah could not stand silently by while the rulers and the people of both Israel and Judah put their faith in armies and alliances, and not in God. To Isaiah it was not important to save the throne or the state. What was important was that people learn to understand the true nature of God.

He warned the Hebrew kings who reigned during his lifetime not to become entangled with Syria, Egypt, Assyria, or the other neighboring powers. The alliances simply introduced more Baalistic ideas and practices into Israel and Judah. Since he felt that Israel and Judah would eventually lose their independence, he gathered together a band of disciples to explain to them the true meaning of God. He wanted to make certain that a remnant of the Hebrews, at least, would understand God.

If only a remnant of such Hebrews remained, said Isaiah, they would be able to build a new nation based on the laws and commandments of God. He promised that such a time would come, when the faithful few, led by a descendant of the House of David, would restore Israel to its homeland as a nation exemplifying justice and righteousness. Then there would follow an era of peace, when people would "beat their swords into plowshares and their spears into pruning hooks; nation shall not lift up sword against nation; neither shall they learn war any more." All the energy that used to go into war and the preparation for war would be applied to the production of things of usefulness and beauty for all mankind to enjoy.

The teaching of Amos, Hosea, and Isaiah inspired some of the Hebrews to write and circulate tracts and pamphlets which crusaded against the impoverishment and enslavement of the poorer Hebrews. These little books pictured

Jahweh as the champion of the downtrodden against the rich. One of these pieces of literature has come down to us as part of the Book of Exodus (20:24 to 23:20). It is generally called the Covenant Code. It implies that the covenant with Jahweh required an end to the charging of interest for loans to needy Hebrews, an end to the foreclosing of mortgages on land, the freeing of Hebrews who had been enslaved for debts after six years. The code also decreed that the fields of wealthy landowners should be left fallow every seventh year, and that the poor were to be permitted to gather whatever crops grew during that year.

The writer of this code was interested in having the Hebrews maintain their independence and social standing as landowners, to prevent their becoming enslaved like the non-Hebrews. We do not know how the code would have worked out, since it was never put into effect, but it is significant that these reforms were suggested in the name of Jahweh. For the first time in human history, religion and ethics (the principles for the decent treatment of others) were becoming identified with each other. The worship of God was being given a new meaning; people were being taught that religion did not mean the appeasement of God in return for some favor, but rather that the worship of God required them to live according to certain rules of conduct in their relations with one another. The rules, moreover, had a new purpose: to insure peace, brotherly love, and security for the individual.

Meanwhile, the Assyrians swooped down upon Israel in 722 B.C. and snuffed out its independence, and when the Assyrians conquered, it was truly a catastrophe. One ancient Assyrian conqueror who left the records of his accomplishments carved on stone, included this gentle recital of one of his battles: he killed 16,000 of the enemy, destroyed the shrines of the enemy god to prove the superiority of the Assyrian god, burned a great many cities, took 1,121 chariots, 470 horses and much other plunder.

They had another gentle custom, the Assyrians. They rounded up the leading citizens of the conquered land, the ruling families, the educated, the skilled craftsmen and artisans, the able and productive people—and carried them captive to their own kingdom. They left no one behind who might attempt to organize a revolt against them. (The Nazis did not usher in a "New Order" as they claimed, when they rounded up millions of civilians in the countries they overran during the Second World War and brought them to work the farms and mines and factories of Germany; they were merely reverting to the cruel practices of the ancient Assyrians, who had destroyed civilizations long before the Nazis.)

The Assyrians carried off the cream of the population of Israel and deposited them in various parts of the Assyrian Empire. No trace of them was ever found, and they are referred to as "the lost ten tribes of Israel." They were never heard of again as Hebrews, probably because they believed that their god had been conquered; and that, to prosper in their new land, they had to worship (live according to the rules of) the superior Assyrian god.

The Assyrians then brought to the land of Israel people from various provinces of their own empire and settled them on the land. Samaria, the capital of the kingdom of Israel, now became the capital of an Assyrian colony, and the people living in it came to be called Samaritans.

A number of Israelites were able to make their way to Judah after the destruction of their kingdom, and they brought to the remaining Hebrew kingdom the books and pamphlets that had been written in Israel. In time the books and legends of the northern kingdom became merged with those of Judah as the common heritage of the Hebrew people.

For a long time Judah had been able to avoid the social process that had brought impoverishment to the Hebrews of Israel, since it was off the main trade routes of Palestine. It was largely pastoral, particularly its southern regions in the Negeb, which bordered on the Arabian desert. Many of the people still lived in tribal communities, pretty much as their ancestors before them had lived in the desert.

However, the western portions of Judah on the seacoast were in the path of the invaders, offering easy access to Egypt in the south or Syria and Babylonia to the north. The Judahites of this section became more and more involved in trade and commerce, dealing directly with non-Hebrew Palestinians and foreigners whose caravans traveled through their cities and whose ships stopped at their ports.

The same social ills that had afflicted Israel began to trouble Judah. A large class of wealthy traders and landowners came into being. The kings of Judah made alliances with neighboring states when Egypt or Assyria or other countries threatened them. Alliances meant tributes to pay, tributes meant heavier burdens of taxation for the people, bringing greater impoverishment for the poor in its wake. Judah became a replica of its sister state, Israel, with its peasantry becoming landless and enslaved. In Judah, too, therefore, voices of protest were heard.

Out of Moresheth, in the lowlands of the southwest along the coastal plain, came another champion of Jahweh, Micah. He was a contemporary of Isaiah and became the mouthpiece of the common man, the peasants of the countryside. For these were the people who were most sorely tried by the frequent wars of the time. He aimed the burden of his message against the wealthy classes of the country, who, he said, spent their time devising ways to oppress the people. Distant Jerusalem, where most of the aristocrats lived, was to him a center of evil, a "town built with blood." He blamed the hardships of the people upon the intrigues of the rulers of the country, the men of wealth of Jerusalem, and upon their disregard for the covenant with Jahweh.

When he heard of the wailing of the rulers because Assyria was attacking and bringing the country great distress, when he heard them cry out that their god had forsaken them, Micah said, no! It was the other way around; *they* had forsaken God. Did the nobles think, asked Micah, that after they gobbled up other people's land and enslaved the poor landowners, God would be pleased with them, simply because they brought fine sacrifices to the Temple? "Will the Lord be pleased with thousands of rams, with tens of thousands of rivers of oil?" Indeed not, said Micah. "It hath been told thee what the Lord doth require of thee; only to do justly and to love mercy, and to walk humbly with thy God."

But the nobles and rulers preferred to believe that rituals and sacrifices were the only way of satisfying Jahweh or any other god. When Judah became a vassal of Assyria, after Israel had been conquered, the rulers introduced, bit by bit, many ritual practices of their conquerors, even erecting shrines to the victorious gods of the foreigners in the hope of gaining their favor, since they believed that Jahweh had forsaken them. For about three-quarters of a century after Micah this process went on, until the religious practices of the Judahites became a confused mass of ceremonies, more foreign than Hebrew.

Some Hebrews of Judah were deeply troubled by this. They, too, wrote tracts and pamphlets to awaken the people to their obligations under the ancient covenant. They attacked, especially, the religious practices instituted by King Manasseh during his long reign, 694–639 B.C., for he had brought into the country the entire Assyrian mode of worship, except that he had placed Jahweh at the head of the Assyrian gods enshrined in the Temple at Jerusalem.

For some time a number of priests of the Temple, inspired by the teaching of the Prophets, made secret plans for the overthrow of the corrupt worship introduced by Manasseh. They sought to replace it with traditional Hebrew worship, and to restore to the land the ancient *mishpat* of the covenant.

The opportunity for the revolution came after Manasseh died and his eight-year-old son, Josiah, succeeded him. The upbringing of the child king was in the hands of the priests, and they developed in him a great respect for Hebrew tradition. They planted a book of laws embodying their ideas in the Temple, which was "discovered" when workers were renovating it. Word was quickly spread that Moses himself had written it, and Josiah made the code the law of the land. This code is largely the legislation in the Book of Deuteronomy, and the attempt to restore the proper wor-

45

ship of Jahweh, under Josiah, is known as the Deuteronomic Reformation.

The Deuteronomic Code sought to displace the rituals of the Palestinian Baals and Assyrian gods, and also attempted to halt the decline of the Hebrew peasantry. It provided for creditors to cancel all unpaid balances of loans after seven years. It forbade the charging of any interest for loans to Hebrews. To make more difficult the foreclosing of a mortgage and the taking of a person's land, it forbade the removal of landmarks, which were stones indicating the family that owned the land; and it commanded the Hebrew not to covet his neighbor's house nor his property.

The Deuteronomic Code (as did the earlier Covenant Code of the Israelites) shows that a strong feeling had developed among the Hebrews that inequality and hardship were repugnant to the nature of their God. The code also reveals how deeply the leaders of the Hebrews had been affected by the religious zeal of the Prophets and their impassioned protests against the immorality of Palestinian life. The writers made the Ten Commandments a part of the Deuteronomic Code in order to root out the murder, stealing, adultery, lying, perjury, and the general disregard for the welfare of others which had become as common in Hebrew life as in the life of their neighbors. The God who had brought the Hebrews out of Egypt, said the Deuteronomic version of the Ten Commandments, was the same God who demanded morality from his worshipers.

But the code could not change the social and economic system of the time. Judah was too much a part of the commercial world, too involved with other nations. Its ruling class, moreover, had no intention of isolating itself, nor of losing any opportunity to increase its wealth and power. When Assyria was under attack by the Babylonian army, King Josiah began to extend his own kingdom northward into the former kingdom of Israel. Then Pharaoh Necho of Egypt invaded Judah and put it under tribute. And then, from the northeast came the thundering hoofs of the mighty Babylonian army of Nebuchadnezzar, who had just conquered Assyria. Judah was now really in trouble.

In those days there lived a man by the name of Jeremiah, a priest of the shrine at Anathoth, in the suburbs three miles out of Jerusalem. He had come to Jerusalem to celebrate one of the great festivals at the Temple, and it grieved him, for he was a man full of pity for his people, to see his countrymen go through the rituals smug and complacent, blinded by their belief that Jahweh lived in the Temple at Jerusalem and would surely protect the city.

Poor deluded people, he said to them; God did not live in that Temple, nor in any other temple. He lived everywhere, said Jeremiah. Just because the Temple stood in Jerusalem did not mean that it and the city were sacred and could not be destroyed. God did not need the Temple, nor even the sacrifices offered there!

To Jeremiah the religion the Hebrews had been practicing was a farce. A man could commit all sorts of crimes —murder, steal, swear falsely against his brothers, oppress and enslave the stranger—and then make his sacrifice at the Temple and feel at peace with God. This was not the way of God. To be at peace with God, a person had to live a good life and perform good deeds. For a people to be at peace, the rulers must govern the land justly: no temple

47

or priests or elaborate cult was needed; God was everywhere, in the wilderness, in the home, but especially in men's hearts. Each person could be his own priest, and only a nation ruled by such people could dwell in safety.

Because of his attacks upon the Temple, with its priests and traditional observances, Jeremiah was put into the public stocks to be jeered at by the people. Later, he was thrown into a pit of quicksand, where he would have perished but for some sympathizers who rescued him. A sentence of death hung over his head almost from the time he began to preach in 627 B.C. The ruling authorities and the priests looked upon him as a dangerous radical who was attacking the very foundation of the state and its religion, and wanted to put him out of the way. But there were many people ready to stand up for Jeremiah; the rulers feared they might bring greater harm on themselves by killing him, since that would make him a martyr and cause his followers to seek revenge. So they persecuted him instead, making his life miserable. In fact, these attacks made him even consider giving up preaching. "It is like a burning fire within my bones," he said. "I strove to withstand it but I could not."

And he continued to preach throughout his long life. He wanted the Hebrews to learn about God so that after the inevitable destruction of Judah, they could remake their religion into one of "inward piety and goodness." That was the true covenant, said Jeremiah, binding God to people, individuals as well as nations.

In 597 B.C., during Jeremiah's lifetime, Nebuchadnezzar's Babylonian army broke into Jerusalem. The Temple was ransacked for its treasures and a number of leading citizens, including members of the royal family, and skilled workers and craftsmen, were carried into exile in Babylonia. The Temple was left standing, but the country was placed under tribute to its Babylonian conquerors.

The Hebrew exiles were distressed. It was bad enough to be uprooted from their homeland and to suffer the hardships of captives in a strange land. But worse than this was to be separated from their god! For Jahweh, they still believed, lived in the Temple at Jerusalem, and how could they worship him in a far-off land? Some of them remembered Jeremiah's words and wrote him to ask what to do in the foreign land in which they now lived.

Jeremiah replied: "Build ye houses, and dwell in them, and plant ye gardens and eat the fruit of them; take ye wives and beget sons and daughters; and take wives for your sons and give your daughters husbands that they may bear sons and daughters; and multiply ye there, that ye be not diminished. . . . For I know the thoughts that I think toward you, saith the Lord: thoughts of peace and not evil, to give you a future and a hope. And ye shall call on Me and find Me, when ye shall search for Me with all your heart."

After the Babylonian attack in 597 B.C., Judah declined rapidly as a country, and its weak rulers could not raise the tribute levied upon them. When Judah stopped sending tribute, Nebuchadnezzar, never one to permit his subjects to flout his authority, laid siege to Jerusalem and, in 586 B.C., once again entered the city. Jerusalem was given over to the Babylonian army for plunder, just as the Japanese during the Second World War handed over the Chinese city of Nanking to its soldiers for three days of loot and rape.

The Temple and the king's palace were stripped of everything valuable and then burned down. The rest of the people of Jerusalem were rounded up and carried captive to Babylon. The kingdom of Judah was no more. No longer was there any Hebrew state in Palestine. The story of the Hebrews as a people seemed to be at an end.

CHAPTER FIVE

The Significance of the Prophets

At this point, 586 B.C., Hebrew history could really have ended. The Israelites had disappeared as a people after the destruction of their state by Assyria in 722 B.C. But the survivors of Judah, after that nation's destruction by Babylonia, did not lose their identity. On the contrary, they were transformed and revitalized; they were made into a new kind of people as a result of the great movement for social justice started by Elijah of Gilead in Israel and carried forward by the great Prophets of Israel and Judah.

Many nations of the Fertile Crescent, Moab, Edom, Philistia, Phoenicia, Assyria, Babylonia, and others, have played their parts on the world stage, and made their exit —finished as a people when they were conquered. Their life as a people depended upon their god who dwelled with them in their land, protecting them and sharing their fate and fortune. When they were conquered they believed their god was vanquished also. They adopted the god of

51

the victorious nation and in time merged with the people whose subjects they had become, completely losing their identity.

These ideas the Hebrews also had held when they lived in Palestine. But the messages of the Prophets, carried into the EXILE by their faithful disciples, completely altered the religious beliefs of the Hebrews. It was an absolutely new concept of God and religion that the Prophets taught: a personal God, needing no temple, spurning gift offerings and sacrifices, which were the very heart of primitive religion. The God of the Prophets lived everywhere, depended upon no specific region for His abode; he was a God who made His bond and covenant with people on the basis of each individual's moral and ethical conduct.

This new religion was not born in a vacuum. It came out of the very life and experience of the Hebrews over hundreds of years. It came as a result of protest, in response to the cry for justice in a world where ancient tribal justice had lost its meaning. For all peoples in their ancient tribal past had had a feeling of justice and equality within the tribe, but it had disappeared when the tribes broke up to live in settled agricultural and commercial communities.

Among the Hebrews too, the sense of tribal justice, of *mishpat*, had begun to weaken after they had settled in Palestine. But so deeply had Moses implanted the idea of *mishpat* in the Hebrew consciousness that it did not die out entirely, especially in the rural areas where the tribal organization had not wholly disintegrated.

The development of rich and poor among the Hebrews, the growth of palaces and slums, of free and slave had aroused Elijah and the Prophets to protest. Inequality, injustice, and immorality existed in every country, but only in Israel and Judah did robust voices link God with the struggle for a better world.

For the good of humanity—not for the Hebrews alone, but for all people—the Prophets wanted to see life reorganized according to the original justice of the tribal past. They attacked, in the name of God, the concentration of wealth in the hands of the few and the consequent degradation of the common man. They decried the placing of profit above human welfare as a denial of God, as a way of life leading to conscienceless, even immoral, exploitation of one's brother.

Thus, as they pleaded for a universal extension of the tribal concept of justice, they developed their new idea of God. They lifted religion and the worship of God above the simple primitive beliefs and practices of the time and gave to religion a noble purpose: to create a world in which life would be more fruitful for all mankind. If everyone could be brought to worship God according to the principles of the covenant, there would be no slavery, no oppression of the poor and needy, but all would get an equitable share of the goods they helped produce. To the Prophets, religion was a way of life that would lead men to greater consideration and helpfulness toward one another. Only among the Hebrews, because of their teaching, did the God become the protector of the poor and needy.

The Prophets delivered their messages with such warmth of language and imagery as to stir their hearers; and their words are alive even today; men in our own time, who work to make the world a better place to live in, still find inspiration in their words and ideas and courage.

Without using the word "democracy," the Prophets were really asking the Hebrews to adopt it as a way of life. Their insistence on the dignity and worth of every individual; their placing of the welfare of God's children above all other considerations; their demand that government exist for the people, not the individual for the state—these are the basic ideas of modern democracy.

Thus, the Prophets gave the Hebrews, and through them the world, a goal to aim for, an ideal to strive for: justice and equality for all mankind. The Prophets visioned the way toward that goal through the new religion they preached, the principal commandments of which prescribed right conduct toward one's fellow men. Other people have since worked toward the same end in other ways. But before the Prophets appeared, men's minds had not been attuned to that goal at all.

These were the ideas that throbbed in the minds of many of the Hebrews who were taken captive to Babylon. Some of them had actually heard Jeremiah in the streets of Jerusalem and been moved by his earnest eloquence. Some had read the writings of the earlier Prophets and their disciples. Many of the survivors took with them stirring legends of the Hebrew struggle for justice. And there were men among them who were impelled to carry forward the movement the Prophets had begun. With enthusiasm they spread their ideas among the Hebrews in exile and welded them into an indissoluble people devoted to the great cause the Prophets had advocated.

CHAPTER SIX

The Establishment of the Jewish Commonwealth

THE captive Hebrews of Judah were a despairing lot, however, when they were first brought to Babylon. They were a subject people uprooted from their land and deprived of their Temple, the dwelling place of their God. Some of the exiles, despite the teachings of the Prophets, adopted the Babylonian gods, in the spirit of the primitive religious notion that every land had its own god. And there was much in Babylonian life to attract the Hebrews, for their captors were an accomplished people, skilled in building, commerce, the arts, and the sciences of astronomy, medicine, and mathematics.

The vast majority of the exiles, however, did not desert Jahweh. They began to meet in one another's homes on the Sabbath to study the books and lore they had brought with them. Increasingly, they came to realize the beauty of the Prophets' conception of God, and they began to feel proud that only among them, among the Hebrews, had this noble idea developed, even though the inequality and injustice that had led the Prophets to preach it were present in every country of the world.

The Hebrews therefore treasured their writings all the more, regarding them as the sacred records of a people who had been honored by God. Their Sabbath get-togethers became so popular that homes could no longer accommodate all of those who wished to participate; special community houses had to be built.

These community houses, which later came to be called synagogues, buzzed with intent talk, for the Hebrews were quite troubled. They did have a new appreciation of Jahweh as a God of love and justice, but how were they to worship Him now that they had no Temple, no priesthood? True, the Prophets had said that priests and sacrifices were not necessary for the worship of God, but they had not offered any substitute forms of worship, and the Hebrews were accustomed to *doing something* to commune with the Deity. How were they to "sing the Lord's song in a strange land?"

They were also quite concerned about their future as a people. Could they establish the new religion in a foreign land? The Prophets had promised them that they would be returned to glory in Palestine some day, led by "the shoot of the stock of Jesse"—in other words, by a descendant of the House of King David. But how could the exiles, a despised and subject people, ever hope to return to Palestine?

But their hopes were raised by a new Prophet who arose among them, Ezekiel, who carried on the great tradition of the earlier Prophets. They would be restored to their ancient homeland, he assured the exiles; God would see to that. It was their destiny to establish in Palestine a perfect commonwealth on earth. That, he said, was the principal aim of the new religion he was teaching them: to build a land in which social justice was enshrined, a country in which people would behave toward one another according to the commandments of God, according to the ethical and moral principles proclaimed by the Prophets. The GENTILES, seeing how peaceful and serene this "nation" would be, would then become worshipers of God, too. Yes, all the world would thus come to the worship of Jahweh as God; they would live in brotherhood, and all the troubles and hardships of the world would be at an end.

In anticipation of the return to Palestine, Ezekiel, in the name of Jahweh, wrote up a constitution for the government of the commonwealth. He provided for a THEOCRACY, a religious state governed by God, in which holy men of perfect character and integrity, true priests, would govern by justly interpreting the Law of God. The king, should the people desire to have one, would be a mere figurehead.

In Ezekiel's commonwealth the land was to be divided up among the people as in the early tribal history of the Hebrews—by lot; and each family's possession was to be protected against seizure, for Ezekiel wanted people to honor the ancient covenant with Jahweh.

Upon their arrival in Palestine, said Ezekiel, the Hebrews were to rebuild the Temple in Jerusalem. To insure proper worship he carefully described the construction of the new Temple and wrote out in detail the rituals and sacrifices to be observed there. His main emphasis in the rituals was upon holiness and purity, his instructions abounding in various rites of purification for Temple services. To Ezekiel the Hebrews were now a holy people, a people consecrated to God. The ancient meaning of the word "holy" was "separate." They were to be "separated"—distinguished—from the other peoples by the ethical and spiritual quality of their lives. He was therefore warning them not to become defiled by contact or association with the heathen gods around them.

Like our own salute to the Flag reminding us of our duty to our country, the Temple rituals and sacrifices were to remind the people of their duty to God, to live justly with their fellow men.

Ezekiel's message had a profound effect upon the Hebrew community in Babylon. They studied his words in their synagogues, looking forward to the time when they would be able to apply them in their own land. They felt the need, meanwhile, to worship, to commune with God. They began to use their synagogues as houses of worship as well as of study. Inspired people among them wrote special prayers and psalms which they recited and sang in unison on the Sabbath. And on the anniversary of the destruction of the Temple, Tishah b'Ab (the ninth day of the Hebrew month of Ab), the exiles met on the shores of rivers and streams in Babylon to utter prayers and laments directly to God. Thus came into existence the first communal prayers of Judaism, a mode of worship requiring no temple or priests.

Their religion, based on the new concept of God, occupied the thoughts of many of the Hebrews. They wanted everything they did to be in keeping with the new ideas. And so, during the Exile, they changed the meaning of the ancient rite of circumcision. In their nomadic past it had been a sort of initiation into the clan, a rite which other Semitic peoples practiced, too. The spiritual leaders of the Exile invested the act of circumcision with a religious significance, making it a symbol of a Hebrew's recognition of the covenant with God. Since the Babylonians did not practice circumcision, it became for the Hebrews a mark of distinction, setting them off as a distinct people. To followers of Ezekiel, this was desirable, for their non-Hebrew neighbors did not believe in the God of the Prophets, and were therefore "heathen" peoples from whom it was necessary to be "separated."

Influenced by Ezekiel, the Hebrews began to regard themselves as a people holy in the eyes of God. The old scrolls and unwritten legends they had brought to Babylon assumed a new significance; they became sacred records of their relationship to God. Scribes and other learned Hebrews recopied the old scrolls and committed to writing some of the old legends. New books and stories, inspired by the Prophets, were also written.

One such story of the Exile period is the beautiful poem about the creation of the world, an elaboration of a Babylonian myth that had excited their imagination. But the Hebrew author changed it to suit the majesty of Jahweh, as the Prophets had described Him, making Him the sole Creator of the earth and all its contents, and of man who was given the earth to rule. Another Hebrew touch was the depiction of God resting from His labors on the seventh day. This was introduced to give added significance to the Sabbath, which was becoming the greatest Holy Day in the Hebrew calendar.

The scribes who copied and recopied the Hebrew scrolls often found material in different scrolls dealing with the same events or customs. For instance, in one of the old scrolls appeared a different story of the creation of man—probably the ancient tradition of the creation as handed down by the southern, Judaic tribes—a more primitive version, in which Jahweh is pictured as molding a bit of clay into the figure of a man and breathing into it to give it life. Some scribe put the two creation stories into the same book. In this way the scribes compiled the various written works of the Hebrews, adding connecting words, sentences, or paragraphs as notes of explanation whenever they came across conflicting stories or obscure references.

The books that the scribes worked on eventually became part of the Hebrew Bible. They were not history books, but rather texts for the teaching of religion in the Babylonian synagogues. It did not matter that they contained contradictory statements here and there, so long as they contained the holy commandments of God.

Five of the books, those dealing with Abraham and the other patriarchs and the life and work of Moses, are called the PENTATEUCH. They were prized by the Hebrews above all others for they contained the most important laws of the new religion. According to a legend that had already taken root among the Hebrews, these books—Genesis, Exodus, Leviticus, Numbers, and Deuteronomy—had been revealed to Moses by God on Mount Sinai. The five books became for the Hebrews the *Torah* (the Teaching); and the Torah became the basis of the new religion, the ethical monotheism the Prophets had developed. It was adherence to the Torah that marked the Hebrews as a people in their Exile, that gave the Hebrews identity, a feeling of national unity even without a homeland.

Many of the exiles, although they accepted the Torah as their guide to the Hebrew way of life, were not satisfied with Ezekiel's insistence upon Palestine as the rightful home of the religion. They also did not like the exclusiveness that his laws of holiness imposed upon them. Many Hebrews had begun to find life comfortable and business profitable in Babylon. They had many contacts with Babylonians which they did not think their religion should interfere with.

They didn't hanker to return to Palestine. After all, Jeremiah and the other Prophets had said that God was everywhere, not just in Jerusalem, and could be worshiped anywhere by observing the rules for ethical conduct. Why must they go to Palestine, even if it should be permitted them some day in the future?

Into the discussion of this problem entered the ideas of another Prophet of the Exile, Isaiah (a second one by that name). The second Isaiah's view was that it was unnecessary for the Hebrews all to return to Palestine. God did not require the temple and rituals Ezekiel had described. According to Isaiah, what was most important in the new religion was that all mankind be brought to recognize Jahweh as the One God of the Universe. That was what God had chosen the Hebrews to do, said he, to unite all the peoples of the earth under God, by teaching them His laws of justice and righteousness. In this sense the Hebrews were the "Chosen People," chosen to be God's servants "to bring forth justice to the nations."

Like the other Prophets, Isaiah regarded justice as equal-

ity, consideration, helpfulness, and brotherly love, virtues
that had been part of the tribal covenant with Jahweh. By
example, the Hebrews were to bring these to the attention
of Gentiles everywhere. They must therefore not withdraw or separate themselves from their non-Hebrew neighbors, but rather live among them so they might the better
carry out the mission God had selected them to perform.

The ideas of Ezekiel and Isaiah developed two conflicting tendencies among the Hebrews of the Exile, one a
drawing-away from the heathen world, the other outward-
looking. These differing attitudes, still present in Jewish
thought, were, nevertheless, both legitimate expressions of
Judaism, since the religion, as it developed from the time
of Ezekiel and Isaiah down to the present, never contained
dogmas, in the sense of beliefs that have a "saving" power,
which one had to accept in order to call oneself a Jew and
to assure one of salvation. Even though the Jews of the
Exile differed in their interpretation of Jewish life and
beliefs, all of them accepted the main purpose of the religion: to apply the ideals of the Prophets to everyday life
and to inspire mankind to establish justice through the acceptance of the One God.

But the precise manner of accomplishing this task was
not clearly defined. To the followers of Ezekiel it meant a
theocracy in Palestine, with a temple and a whole body of
rituals. To them it meant that the Hebrews must become an
exclusive, holy people. The Ezekielites therefore devised
various ceremonies and laws to keep themselves distinct
from their neighbors, in fact apart from them, lest they be
defiled by contact with the "unclean." They feared such
contact would lead to imitation of the ungodly behavior of

the heathens. They developed dietary laws prohibiting the use of certain animals, not mainly because they were harmful to health, but also because they were sacred to other religions. They outlawed intermarriage, which had been practiced among the Hebrews from time immemorial, as a danger to the religion and a block to the proper observance of the rituals.

The followers of Isaiah stressed instead ethical and moral conduct and sought contact with their neighbors as a means of spreading the new religion. They did not favor withdrawing into themselves as a people apart.

While the exiles were thus deeply engrossed in religious thought, the Persians, led by Cyrus the Great, conquered the Babylonians. Whereas other emperors controlled their subject peoples through force, even to the point of transplanting whole populations, Cyrus believed it more advisable to permit the conquered peoples to continue their traditional way of life in their homelands. They would then have less cause to revolt.

In keeping with this idea, he issued a decree in 538 B.C., giving the Hebrews the right to return to their ancient homeland, to rebuild their Temple and settle in the land. He offered them an escort of Persian soldiers to ensure their safety along the six hundred miles they would have to travel.

There was great excitement among the exiles. To them it was nothing short of proof that God had intervened in their behalf, for had not Ezekiel and Isaiah promised that God would arrange their return? But it was now more than a generation since the beginning of the Exile, and there were a great many Hebrews who had no personal memories of Palestine, and who, therefore, felt no particular attachment to it. They were content to remain in Babylon, under Persian rule, where they could worship God just as well, and where they felt quite at home. Only about forty-five thousand of them took advantage of Cyrus' offer and left for Jerusalem, to build the Temple there as the center of the perfect commonwealth devoted to God.

When they arrived in Jerusalem, they found the ancient Temple a mass of ruins, the walls of the city in need of extensive repair, and the land waste. They were met by the Samaritans and other Hebrews who had been living in and around the city. These people, true to their primitive god-of-the-land religion, were worshipers of Jahweh, but not in the same way the returned exiles worshiped God. The Samaritans clung to the ancient Hebrew forms of worship and to the ways of life that had obtained in the land before the destruction of the Temple. They were pleased that the newcomers were going to rebuild the Temple, which to them meant simply the abode of Jahweh, and offered their help.

The returning pioneers, however, regarded the Samaritans and native Hebrews as idol worshipers with whom they could have no contact, else the holiness of the Temple would be completely defiled. So they notified the Samaritans that they could not accept their offer; that, in fact, the Temple was not for them at all, since they were not true worshipers of God. This infuriated the Samaritans, who believed that they were being denied access to the new home of their god.

To make life miserable for the newcomers, they sent word to the Persian governor that the Babylonian Hebrews were fortifying Jerusalem with the purpose of defying Persian rule, and that they had even selected a man by the name of Zerubbabel, a descendant of the House of David, as their king. Actually, Zerubbabel was only the civil head of the community, a figurehead as the constitution of Ezekiel had directed.

The Persians ordered an end to all building operations. This made the Samaritans bolder, and they, along with other natives, attacked the newly-organized community. On top of this, the pioneers also suffered from droughts and locust plagues. All this caused many of them to seek safety and security among the Hebrew colonies in and around Jerusalem. They married into native Hebrew families and began to live and worship like their in-laws and neighbors.

The reduced band of the faithful appealed to Persia and finally got permission to continue work on the Temple. Spurred on by the exhortations of their religious leaders, Haggai and Zechariah, they completed their task in 518 B.C., about twenty years after their arrival. It was not as expensive and wonderful a building as the Temple of King Solomon. But it was a Temple built by the blood and sweat of a people fired by religious zeal; a Temple for worship, not for show.

Their neighbors, believing themselves Hebrew kinsmen of the returned exiles, smarted at the exclusiveness of the pioneers, and regarded their insistence on keeping the Temple holy as an affront to them. They attacked the new community again and again. The beautiful dream that had lured the exiles from Babylon was turning into a nightmare in Jerusalem.

Meanwhile, in the Babylonian regions of the Persian Empire, the large Hebrew communities continued to study and pray in their synagogues, and their faith grew stronger. A few generations after the first batch of exiles had returned to Jerusalem, a Babylonian religious leader by the name of Ezra decided to come to Jerusalem to see Mount Zion on which the Temple stood. When it became known that Ezra was making the pilgrimage to Zion, a number of Hebrews decided to join him, and Ezra led some sixteen hundred Hebrews from various parts of Babylon to Jerusalem.

What Ezra found upon his arrival was indeed distressing. The observance of the Sabbath was being neglected; the laws of the faith were being disregarded; the wealthy were oppressing the poor; people had lost their land and had become enslaved. He tore his garments, as a sign of mourning, and threw himself to the ground and wept. He called God to witness that he was ashamed at the way His people were living. Ezra's grief was so heart-rending that the people wept with him, feeling that they had committed grievous sins.

Ezra commanded all the Hebrews to appear before him, to be instructed in the laws of God, under penalty of exclusion from the community and loss of all property. He ordered them to give up their heathen wives and abandon the practices of the surrounding peoples. They were to observe only the Torah, the word of God as revealed to Moses, which Ezra had brought with him from Babylon.

A great many did send away their foreign wives, an act which brought the community new troubles, for the surrounding peoples regarded this as a grave insult to them. Coupled with Ezra's insistence on purging the community of any contact with heathen ways, it looked as if the followers of the Torah considered themselves a superior people. The neighbors were outraged anew and again attacked the Temple and the community.

The deteriorating conditions in Jerusalem came to the ears of a wealthy Persian Hebrew by the name of Nehemiah, a high official in the court of Artaxerxes I, the ruler of the Persian Empire. He obtained a leave of absence from his king, that he might come to the aid of his co-religionists. Armed with a royal letter to the Persian governors around the province of Judea, of which Palestine was a part, to supply him with necessary building materials, Nehemiah set out for Jerusalem in the year 445 B.C.

He came to the city unannounced, to study the problems and needs of the community, after which he made himself known, presenting his credentials from the king. He organized the Hebrews into battalions and set them to work strengthening the city walls to make it safe from attack. He kept after them until Jerusalem was completely fortified.

Nehemiah then called a special meeting to give the people a report on the observations he had made. It was actually a severe lecture, for he was dissatisfied with the way the community was operating. There were too many among them with no land at all, and too many who were wealthy, even though they had all started out equal when they came from Babylon. He blamed this inequality on their departure from the laws of the Torah; some people were not treating their fellow Hebrews justly, as the religion required. He pointed out to them that it was against the laws of the Torah to make the needy pay interest on loans, to confiscate the land of those who could not repay their loans, or to enslave a fellow Hebrew.

They must separate themselves from the ungodly, Nehemiah told them, lest they fall into the error of their ways. It was imperative that they observe, with the utmost strictness, the laws of the Torah.

The wealthy nobles of the city did not like his lecture, but the majority of the people were on his side. He set an example of kindness and consideration by canceling all debts owed him by people who had borrowed money and supplies from him during the rebuilding of the walls. And because the harvest had been a poor one, he distributed grain free to the needy and made no tax collections for the upkeep of his office as governor.

To make the city stronger, Nehemiah built homes and called in Hebrews from the surrounding villages. He ordered the gates of the city closed on the Sabbath, to prevent the Lord's day from being profaned by contact with heathens. He arranged a system of taxation for the upkeep of the Temple and the priests. He broke up all groups not in sympathy with the ideas of the perfect commonwealth, even expelling grumbling nobles and faithless priests.

Nehemiah's love for the Torah profoundly impressed the Hebrews, and made the work of Ezra considerably easier. The people listened avidly as he read and explained the Torah to them. Many copies of the Torah and other sacred writings such as the Books of the Prophets began to circulate in Judea. Schools for the study and discussion of the religion were established. The people accepted the Torah as the loving word of God; in fact, from this time on each

Over the years these ideas became interwoven with Jewish thought, blending with Jewish beliefs of similar vein.

The Persians, for instance, believed in angels who did the will of their god, Ahura-Mazda. This notion appealed to a number of Jews. They had an exalted view of God; the angel concept made it possible further to exalt Him. With angels to act as intermediaries in His dealings with human beings, God could remain holy and pure, uncontaminated by concern with the petty details of mere mortals.

The Persians believed, also, that Ahura-Mazda rewarded the faithful after death, in a future world. This idea occasioned much discussion in the Jewish schools and caused a change in Jewish thought concerning the hereafter. The Jews had never paid much attention to the hereafter, being concerned mainly with establishing justice on earth. In their Hebrew past, they had believed that the soul, after death, simply went to a great cavern under the earth, *Sheol*, there to continue its existence.

The Prophets had spoken of a "Day of the Lord," when the Hebrew *nation* would be restored and made supreme under the leadership of the "Messiah"—God's anointed one. Jeremiah and Ezekiel, however, had stressed the *individual's* relationship with God. To this was added the Persian emphasis on *individual* reward and punishment. Jews began to talk about the restoration of the individual soul to its body after death, its resurrection in the day of the Messiah to enjoy the peace he would bring to *all* humanity on earth in the Day of Judgment.

The Jews did not reject an idea just because it was foreign. If it had value, and if its values could be harmonized with the spirit of the Torah and the Prophets, it was regarded as Jewish, no matter what its origin may have been. And so the blended ideas went into the storehouse of Jewish speculations about life and death.

Toward the end of the Persian period a slight change in the emphasis of Judaism also began to manifest itself. In the days of the Prophets, much stress had been put on equality as one of the goals of social justice. In those days, there was still a certain amount of tribal life among the Hebrews. They were not at the time far removed from the communal spirit of the tribe. But in Judea under the Persians the Jews no longer lived as members of tribes or clans; they were individuals in settled communities and thought in terms of their own individual welfare. Many religious leaders no longer regarded inequality of wealth as in itself a departure from the covenant. The emphasis was on just and honest dealing with one another, on kindness and consideration for one another in business and human relations.

The comparative peace and quiet in the Jewish community came to an end shortly after 332 B.C., the year in which Alexander the Great, the famous leader of the Greeks, conquered Persia and took possession of Judea. After Alexander's death, the Greek Empire was divided into three parts and Judea became a province of the Greek-ruled Syrian Empire.

When the Greeks, a nation of merchants, manufacturers, and traders, conquered a land, Greeks were encouraged to settle in the new territory to open it up for trade and commerce. Greece itself was a mountainous and rocky country, with limited facilities for good farming. Many

Greeks, therefore, left their homeland for the provinces.

When the Greeks settled anywhere in those days, they brought with them their culture, the product of their great writers, artists, thinkers, musicians, and builders. They modeled their new cities according to the pattern of the homeland; their buildings were done in Greek style; they built theaters and gymnasiums for the spectacles and games they loved. They brought in their language, their books, and their gods.

All over Palestine a number of such Greek communities mushroomed. Many Jews had frequent contact with them, for they did much business with the Greeks. When Jews entered Greek communities they were charmed by the customs and manners, by the very spirit of the Greeks. Many Jews began to speak Greek and to read Greek books. They also dressed like the Greeks and gave their children Greek names. As a matter of fact, a rather large number of Jews who had settled in the Grecian city of Alexandria, in Egypt, became so Hellenized (so like the Greeks) that the Torah had to be translated for them into Greek so they could learn to understand its laws.

Being captivated by Greek life involved more than merely adopting Greek manners and customs. The Greeks were polytheists, as the Hebrews of old had been; they believed in many gods and dedicated their public buildings, their games and spectacles to those gods. So when Jews attended Greek theatrical performances, or participated in their sports events, they were in effect honoring foreign gods, thus breaking the commandment to worship only God.

The Jews who mingled with the Greeks were led to

break other commandments, such as the strict observance of the Sabbath and the prohibition against eating non-Kosher foods ("unclean" for Jews). Some of these commandments were not in the Torah; they had come into Jewish life as a result of the interpretations of the Torah that the learned schoolmasters and elders of the community had made from time to time. For the Holy Scriptures had been written centuries before and did not deal specifically with every new situation Jews had to face. When problems arose Jewish religious leaders discussed them in the light of the WRITTEN LAWS of the Torah. By applying the spirit of the Torah, they arrived at new regulations to cover the specific situation. These decisions were called the ORAL LAW, and were studied in the schools along with the Torah, the Written Law, thus becoming part of the religious tradition of the Jews. Most people accepted them as extensions of the Torah, in the same way that Americans accept as the law of the land the decisions and interpretations of the Constitution made by the Supreme Court.

The makers of the Oral Law felt it their duty to build a "fence around the Torah," to make rules that would keep the religion pure and the people holy, "separated" from the polytheistic beliefs and practices of their neighbors. But Jews who associated with Greeks often dined with them, which meant partaking of foods prohibited by the religious leaders. And they often dealt with Greeks on the Sabbath, which the Greeks did not observe as a Holy Day, although the interpreters of the Torah had prohibited the carrying on of any business on the Sabbath as a profanation of the Law.

Contact with the Greeks also meant contact with Greek

literature and Greek philosophic ideas, as a result of which many Jews were weakened in their religious faith; some Jews even became skeptics, if not total unbelievers.

So it was with a mounting sense of horror that the pious elders watched the process of Hellenization of the Jews. Fearing that the attractive festivals and merrymaking of the Greeks would draw Jews away from the synagogue and Temple, they made more stringent rules to keep the Jews away from the Greeks, outside of absolutely necessary business contacts. But not all Jews were willing to obey these rules; and there was no way at that time to enforce the decisions. The Oral Laws were not binding, their only authority coming from the respect the Jews had for their religious leaders.

The Hellenist Jews accepted the laws of the Torah but they regarded the new interpretations as unnecessarily strict and confining. They wanted to live an honest and good life and enjoy it at the same time. They saw nothing wrong in participating in Greek life, for the statues and idols of the Greek gods really meant nothing to them. The Greeks could worship them if they wanted to; they themselves, the Hellenized Jews, worshiped God at the Temple.

But this was wrong in the eyes of a great many Jews. Like Ezekiel, they felt Jewish life must place piety above all else, must be uncontaminated by heathen practices. The Pious Ones, or Hasidim as they came to be called, wanted all Jews to differentiate themselves sharply from the Greeks and from the Hellenized Jews as well. They showed their dislike for the Hellenists by wearing, as far as possible, ancient Hebrew costumes, in contrast to the elegant Grecian clothes. They shunned everything Grecian.

The Hasidim were not simply fanatics or killjoys; they were objecting to the watering-down of Jewish life and faith, particularly because it was the aristocratic priests, the traders, and businessmen who had become Hellenized. Besides Greek customs and manners, they had adopted sharp business practices and an intense pursuit of wealth and pleasure, with a resulting disregard for the Jewish moral code and for the welfare of others. The Hasidim, on the contrary, were trying to re-emphasize the virtues the Prophets had preached.

Not all the Jews were either Hasidim or Hellenists. There were many who recognized that there was much in Greek life that was praiseworthy, but they did not think it necessary to stray from the path of the Prophets to enjoy the richer life.

In a way it was a healthy state of affairs for differences of opinion to exist among the Jews. The discussions prevented their religion from becoming static, so fixed that it could not progress with changing conditions. It was only natural for disagreements to occur, since Ezekiel and the second Isaiah themselves had disagreed as to Jewish practices and ideas. Jews felt free to roam unrestricted all over the intellectual horizon in their search to understand the Word of God, as long as they traveled along the route of the Prophets and the Torah. They felt free to accept those interpretations of the religion which were most convincing to them, most expressive of the teachings of the Prophets and the Torah. So long as Judea enjoyed self-government the quarrels of the Hellenists and the Hasidim presented no danger to the commonwealth.

This division among the Jews became a distinct danger,

however, when Antiochus Epiphanes, in the year 175 B.C., became the Greek ruler of Syria, the empire of which Judea was a part. For he was a king with delusions of grandeur, who yearned to enlarge his empire and have all his subjects worship him as a god, as the Greeks did.

To supply his large armies, Antiochus appointed tax collectors for various regions, collecting from them a fixed amount of money beforehand. The officials then taxed the people of the region, keeping as profit for themselves whatever they got above the amount they paid Antiochus for the job. It was a wonderful opportunity for greedy persons to make a fortune, and men of wealth competed against each other for the jobs by offering higher sums to the king. Naturally, the larger the sum paid to Antiochus, the heavier were the taxes levied on the people.

The wealthier Jews became active Hellenists to win the favor of Antiochus. One of them, a man by the name of Jason, got himself appointed to the position of high priest in return for a large bribe. The Hasidim became aroused, for the Jewish leaders had always selected the high priest. They objected to the action of Antiochus as an encroachment on their communal independence, as an interference in their internal affairs.

When, a few years later, a Jew by the name of Menelaus offered Antiochus a greater bribe, the king removed Jason from the high priesthood and installed Menelaus as his successor. This was, to the Hasidim, a heinous crime, not mere meddling in their internal affairs; for Menelaus was not even related to the family from which traditionally the high priests were selected. The Jews attacked Menelaus when

Antiochus was busy on distant battlefields, and drove him from the Temple.

Antiochus was furious when he heard of the attack. He began to look upon the Jews as a troublesome and rebellious lot, too unlike his other subjects; they did not respect him enough, and they refused to worship him as a god. He could not permit them to flout his authority, lest his other subjects take heart and do likewise. Since it was their religion that made them act that way, he decided to make war on Judaism, to force the Jews to abandon their faith and become completely Greek in observance and spirit.

The army he ordered to Jerusalem entered the city on the Sabbath. The pious Jews refused to fight or even defend themselves on that sacred day, fleeing instead to the suburbs of the city and the hills beyond, but not before the Greeks had slaughtered several thousand of them. The treasures of the Temple were carted off for Antiochus, and the city was left in the hands of the leading Hellenists, with whom Antiochus felt he could do business. He ordered a statue of Zeus placed in the Temple, to convert it into a Greek shrine. He decreed the observance of the Sabbath a grave crime, and forbade, under pain of death, the practice of the Jewish dietary laws. And just because they were "unclean" animals, Antiochus ordered the regular sacrifice of pigs on the Temple altar. Everything possible was done to wipe out all trace of Judaism.

The small band of Hellenists did not find Antiochus' attack on Judaism painful. But among the pious Jews an underground movement developed. In caves, in hills, wherever they could hide from the spying eyes of the Greeks, the Hasidim worshiped, studied and carried on their religion. It was dangerous to be a Jew, but thousands braved it.

Antiochus sent his troops all over Judea to erect Greek shrines and to force the Jews to sacrifice forbidden animals to the Greek gods. When the soldiers came to the town of Modin, near Jerusalem, the Greeks met a kind of resistance they did not expect.

In that village lived an old man by the name of Mattathias. He and his five sons were among the populace that had been ordered to appear at the Greek shrine. The soldiers commanded the Jews to perform the Greek sacrificial ceremony. When one of the Jews stepped up to the altar to sacrifice the swine the Greeks had prepared, Mattathias lunged fiercely at the Jew and ran him through with his sword. He and his sons then turned on the Greek soldiers, hacking away. The Greek band was routed, and Mattathias called on the Jews to follow him to the hills in the name of the Lord. Thus was begun the Jewish rebellion against Antiochus.

Many Jews made their way to the hills and mountains, where Mattathias and his sons organized them into guerrilla fighters to harass the soldiers of Antiochus wherever they could. When Mattathias died, one of his sons, Judah "Maccabee" (the "Hammer"), took over the leadership of the growing army of Jews.

Fighting with zeal, for God and the right to live as Jews, Judah's army, after three years, drove the Greeks out of Jerusalem. The first task he set his men was to purify the Temple, to make it Jewish once more. When it was once again fit for Jewish worship, Judah decreed an eight-day festival period of rededication. So began the Hanukkah festival which Jews all over the world still celebrate in honor of the victory of the Maccabees. It thus commemorates the first known war for religious freedom in the history of the world, a war in which the Jews defended their right to practice their religion according to their own beliefs, and to follow the customs and traditions that had grown up among them.

Although the Jews had recaptured only Jerusalem, Antiochus decided to come to terms with them, for he was occupied in a number of wars elsewhere and had to relieve the strain on his hard beset armies. So, in the year 165 B.C., he granted the Jews religious freedom and communal independence within his empire.

The Hasidim, who had formed the backbone of the resistance, were satisfied. They had no desire to continue the struggle for complete independence, for a king of their own. Their main aim, to safeguard Judaism and its way of life under the Torah, had been achieved. The Hasidim, therefore, ended their war against Antiochus, repaired to the countryside to rebuild their synagogues and schools, and to root out all vestiges of Greek religion that Antiochus had introduced.

The official head of the Jewish community was still the high priest. Even though Ezekiel's constitution had provided for a figurehead king (like the modern king of England), the Jews had never appointed one. From the start of the new commonwealth, the priests had served both as the civil and religious heads of the community; as interpreters of the Law and as guardians of the Temple cult and rituals.

The administrative body of the commonwealth was the

SANHEDRIN, a sort of supreme court empowered to decide cases on the basis of the Torah. The high priest was its president and selected the members of the Sanhedrin from among the leading priests and educated laymen of the community. As head of the Sanhedrin, the high priest was actually the chief authority in the Jewish commonwealth. The leader of the Jews in 165 B.C. was Jonathan, a brother of Judah Maccabee; but he was not the high priest since he was not of the traditional high priestly family.

Shortly after the end of the rebellion, the Syrian Empire became involved in civil war as a result of the seizure of the throne by Alexander Balas. In an attempt to get the backing of the province of Judea, Alexander Balas had offered Jonathan the office of high priest. Jonathan, ambitious for personal power, accepted. Although some extremists among the Hasidim grumbled, Jonathan was hailed by the people, so popular were the Maccabees.

While the Syrians were weak because of internal strife, Jonathan made war against various Syrian generals to gain a greater degree of independence for the commonwealth, battles in which he was successful. This turn of affairs was distasteful to the Hasidim; they disliked having politics mixed up with the holy office of high priest. They preferred their high priest to be divorced from state affairs and the struggle for power; they wanted the high priest to devote himself entirely to the administration of the Torah.

Jonathan's successor, Simon, continued Jonathan's work of making Palestine politically independent. But he did not stop after he had won freedom from Syrian rule. For by this time a considerable class of merchants and traders had grown up among the Jews, men who conducted large import and export businesses. There were also wealthy landowners who had vast estates where grapes, olives, spices, and other products were grown, crops that could be sold far and wide. They were all interested in expanding their trade. They therefore encouraged Simon to embark upon a series of campaigns against other nations in Palestine, and he made a number of conquests, particularly of ports on the Mediterranean Sea.

The men behind Simon were interested primarily in creating a powerful Jewish state, in expanding the national territory and in promoting opportunities for trade. To further these ends they organized themselves into the Sadducee Party, to back the political activities of the Hasmoneans, as the members of the Maccabee family were called. The prophetic ideal of a religious commonwealth based on social justice was a secondary consideration with them. For them, the essence of Judaism was the proper conduct of the Temple services, in accordance with the Written Law of the Torah.

Because the Hasmoneans and their Sadduceean backers busied themselves with political matters, the pious among the Jews began to feel that the commonwealth was becoming just another state, like those ruled by neighboring kings. The Jewish rulers were adopting Greek manners and dress, and were continually increasing their power and wealth, disregarding the gradual impoverishment of the common people which the Hasmonean wars and the high taxes necessary to conduct them were causing.

The Jews for whom the spiritual ideals of the religion were of paramount importance now organized themselves in opposition to the Sadducees, to revive the idea of the commonwealth the Prophets had preached about. They formed themselves into a brotherhood, or fraternity, which became known as the Pharisees. Their watchword was strict observance of the laws of ritual and moral purity. They did not oppose the Temple and its cult; they simply felt that, by itself, the Temple could not create the perfect commonwealth, especially since it was presided over by Sadduceean priests who disregarded the Oral Law. The Pharisees wanted every phase of life to be Jewish, to reflect the teachings of the religion.

In 134 B.C., an event occurred that caused the Pharisees great concern. In that year, John Hyrcanus, who had become high priest upon the death of his father, Simon, declared himself king of the country. To the Pharisees, a king who exercised both religious and political power would surely use his religious position mainly to enhance his secular interests. Besides, a Jewish king, they felt, should come from the House of David, for this had long been the traditional expectation among the Jews, and John Hyrcanus was not of that royal line.

Despite the opposition of the Pharisees, John Hyrcanus went merrily on his kingly way. He conquered Samaria and Edom, and forced the people of these countries to adopt Judaism, for as Jews they would have to accept him both as their secular king and religious head. The Hasmonean kings who followed John added to his conquests, until they built up an empire larger than the one King David had ruled.

The Pharisees began to find increasing support among the common people. The workers of the city and countryside had gained nothing from the wars and conquests. In fact, their poverty and discontent had increased. Only a spark was needed to drive many of them to rebellion. The spark was provided by the actions of the tyrannical Alexander Jannaeus, who came to the throne about the year 102 B.C.

Besides keeping up continual, costly war against various Greek cities, Alexander Jannaeus committed a breach of the religious law by marrying Salome, his brother's widow, although the Torah expressly forbade the high priest to marry a widow. During a Holy Day service, when Alexander Jannaeus was officiating as high priest at the Temple, he came to that part of the service which required him to pour a water libation on the altar, a ritual that had been introduced at the insistence of the Pharisees. To show his contempt for the Pharisees, who had been instigating the people against him, he deliberately poured the water at his feet. The people were so angered by this flagrant disregard for the law that they threw the ceremonial palm branches and citrons they were holding right at the king.

The resentment against the king rose to such heights that an armed revolt broke out against him. Alexander Jannaeus put down the rebellion of his people with great cruelty; and when he had the country under his control again, he ordered a massacre of the Pharisees.

In 75 B.C., when Alexander Jannaeus died and his wife Salome Alexandra succeeded him to the throne, she appointed her son Hyrcanus to the office of high priest. Hyrcanus appointed many Pharisees to the Sanhedrin which, up to that moment, had been controlled by the Sadducees. The Pharisees were now in a position to influence both the religious and civil heads of the common-wealth.

The Pharisees believed that all Jews, of high and low estate, must apply to every activity in their lives the law and spirit of the Torah. In order to spread the knowledge of the Jewish faith among the people, so that all Jews would know its rules and commandments, the Pharisees enacted a law that had far-reaching effects upon the Jews. By it, for the first time in the history of the world, the education of children was made compulsory. The law required that every town or village with ten or more families must furnish at least one teacher for every twenty-five children. They thus established the principle that learning and study were important adjuncts to religious expression. They started many adult academies to train teachers, and since these schools were all part of the synagogue organization, the Pharisees thus made the synagogue the dominant institution in Jewish life, around which the entire life of the community revolved.

When Queen Salome Alexandra died, Hyrcanus, the high priest, sought to become king. The Sadducees opposed him, preferring his younger brother, Aristobulus, who was a Sadducee. Some of the leaders of the Pharisees were ready to back Hyrcanus, but most of them were alienated by his desire for the throne. A civil war broke out in the common-wealth, with Hyrcanus and Aristobulus leading opposing armies.

Meanwhile, new world conquerors, the Romans, had made their appearance in Asia Minor. Aristobulus sent envoys to the Roman commander in chief, Pompey, offering Palestine as a vassal state of Rome, if Pompey would recognize him as king. Hyrcanus also sent representatives to Pompey with the same proposal, except that Hyrcanus be the king. Pompey must have become bewildered when a third group of Jews came to see him, the Pharisees, who wanted no king at all. They wanted him to establish a council of elders to rule the community, with a guarantee that the people would have the right to live under their Torah, as Jews.

Pompey, however, had his own solution to the problem of Palestine, the conqueror's solution. He divided the country, in order to weaken it, into provinces and the provinces into districts. He appointed as governor of the province of Judea a man by the name of Antipater, a Jew from Edom, the country that had been forced into Judaism by an earlier Hasmonean king. He was to be responsible to Rome, not to the Sanhedrin, which was stripped of political power. Pompey made no attempt to tamper with the religious life of the Jews, leaving Hyrcanus in his position of high priest and head of the Sanhedrin.

Many Jews resented the idea of becoming puppets of Rome and tried to prevent Pompey's legions from entering Jerusalem, but their resistance was of no avail. The Romans drowned it in blood, plundered the city and took many captives to sell as slaves. The Jews returned to their daily tasks, licking their wounds. They had had their first taste of Roman rule and policy. They still had communal freedom; but they themselves felt that they were now not even as free as they had been under Persian or Greek Rule.

CHAPTER EIGHT

Under the Roman Eagle

NO section of the Roman Empire was permitted to feel free, the Roman rulers keeping all their subjects under continual supervision. They regarded their conquered territories merely as sources of wealth in the form of taxes, slaves, and trade. They organized them so as to keep steady the flow of riches from every section of their vast empire, always holding garrisons in readiness at strategic points to put down even the first sign of rebellion.

The rulers built fine highways that fanned out from Rome in all directions, to promote commerce and to police the empire. In this way, Imperial Rome was able for long periods to keep its subjects quiet; but it was the quiet of a well-guarded prison. As soon as the Romans became engaged in any large-scale battle and had to call in reinforcements from one or another of the provinces, the peoples in the freshly undermanned areas made a break for freedom. For Roman rule was harsh and burdensome, punishment for infractions swift and bloody, and people simply did not relish living as virtual prisoners.

Conditions were pretty much the same all over the empire and, like other subject peoples, the Jews also champed at the bit. There were over two million Jews in Palestine and the vast majority of them were finding it increasingly difficult to make a living. The high taxes were draining their resources; the Roman military garrisons were consuming their substance; and greedy Roman officials were snatching up everything they could get their hands on. No sooner did a Jewish farmer harvest his crop than the grasping hands of tax collectors started digging into it. Before they were through with him he had practically nothing left to sell or to live on.

Farms were saddled with mortgages, and more and more mortgages were being foreclosed. While some Jerusalem Jews, who played hand in glove with the Roman rulers, became owners of vast estates in the countryside, many Jews became landless. Some of them became sharecroppers or slaves, while others drifted to the towns and cities.

The Jewish artisans in the towns and cities had their problems too. They not only had to pay high taxes, but they were also in competition with the non-Jewish artisans of the nearby Greek cities, whose products were beginning to flood the Jewish communities. The dispossessed Jews coming from the rural areas simply made a bad situation worse. People in general had little money, so the increased production glutted the market with goods, thus forcing prices down. Few artisans could make enough to remain in business. Unemployment increased, and a considerable number of Jews became poverty-stricken.

The Roman government did not directly interfere in the domestic affairs of the Jews, nor were the emperors interested in their plight. All the rulers wanted was that the governors of the conquered territories keep the tribute flowing into their coffers, and the subject peoples in check. And Antipater, appointed to govern the Roman province of Judea, "filled the bill" perfectly. He governed Judea not as a Jew but as a Roman official, seeing to it that all the required taxes were collected and that all opposition, either to himself or to Rome, was put down.

Some Jews made for the hills and mountains to carry on guerrilla warfare against the Romans, particularly in the district of Galilee, which was governed by one of Antipater's sons, Herod. Jews who abominated Rome regarded these "partisans" as heroes; to the Romans they were treasonous outlaws. Herod therefore hunted the "rebels" and summarily executed those he captured. Jews of Galilee and elsewhere were angered by Herod's and Antipater's quisling-type loyalty to Rome.

Meanwhile, Rome itself became involved in civil war. Julius Caesar, the Roman dictator, was assassinated and a number of Roman generals fell to fighting among themselves, each trying to establish himself as ruler. The resulting confusion was welcomed by those Jews who yearned for freedom. Antigonus, of the Hasmonean family, raised a Jewish army. He got help from the Parthians, as the people of the Persian Empire were then called; for the Parthians were eager to drive the Romans out of the area and thus end the threat to their independence. Together they attacked and defeated the Roman garrison. Antigonus tracked down Antipater, killing him and all his sons except

Herod, who happened at that very time to be on his way to Rome on some official business. In the year 40 B.C., Antigonus declared himself king of Judea.

After the civil war within Rome had ended, the Roman Senate turned its attention again to its colonial empire. Impressed by Herod, the Senate appointed him king of the Jews, to rule Judea in the name of Rome. A bitter war ensued between Antigonus and Herod, during which the city of Jerusalem was practically destroyed and many Jews lost their lives. In 37 B.C., with the aid of Roman legions, Herod finally won out and installed himself as the new king.

Herod's main interest was in statecraft; he tried to please all elements in his domain, the Greeks, the Jews, but most of all his Roman masters. He built a city on the Mediterranean, Caesarea, in honor of Augustus Caesar, the Roman emperor. He built palaces and fortresses, temples and amphitheaters for Greeks and Romans. He kept the highways and ports safe for commerce. Trade again began to flow into the country, and business improved.

He rebuilt Jerusalem and converted some marshy areas into fertile farming regions. He rebuilt the old Temple so magnificently that it became one of the wonders of the ancient world. The only trouble with the Temple was that Herod had a golden eagle, the symbol of Rome, mounted on its front gate. To the Jews the eagle was normally a hateful symbol of oppression; but on the gate of the Temple it was a goading, maddening sight, for it was to the pious a sacrilegious idol, making the Temple a heathen shrine.

Herod had done this not to infuriate the Jews but to

please his Roman masters, since he needed their help to maintain his power and wealth. Nevertheless, he was often quite considerate of the Jews too. When unemployment and famine brought suffering to great numbers of the people, he remitted some of the taxes he had collected, and even provided relief out of his own funds. This, too, was simply statecraft—he wanted no gnawing discontent in the land that might lead the Jews to rebel.

From Herod's point of view statecraft was all-important, but to most of the Jews the religious life of the commonwealth was far more important. The Pharisees, particularly, disliked Herod's lack of respect for Jewish religious ideals and practices; for this reason a group of them one day ripped the golden eagle from the Temple gate. In retaliation Herod ordered a little massacre to teach the pious Jews not to interfere with his state policies.

To the Pharisees, rulers like Herod were making Judea just another kingdom, neither better nor worse than the neighboring ones. The ideal of the perfect commonwealth, as taught by Ezekiel, and the just world, as visioned by Isaiah, were being pushed into the background. As far as Herod was concerned, the Oral Law the Pharisees had been developing out of the discussions in the schools was mere talk and speculation. To him and the ruling classes, Judaism meant little more than the performance of those Temple rituals specifically written down in the Torah. They did not recognize any other law or tradition.

The Pharisees, the inheritors of the zeal of Ezra and Nehemiah, however, wanted the Jews by every thought and act to glorify God, to strive to attain His moral perfection and thus bring true justice into the life of the nation, and humility and mercy into everyday conduct. They wanted Judea to become a shining example for all the world to behold and emulate. For this, no king was needed; no conquests, no state power. Only the good life, as prescribed by those learned in the Law, was necessary to usher in the Messianic time Jews looked forward to, the day when all mankind would come to the worship of the One God. So long as Rome did not interfere in the internal affairs of the commonwealth all this was possible, the Pharisees felt; provided, of course, that the leaders of the Jewish community stopped dabbling in politics and dedicated themselves to the task the Prophets had set for the Jews.

Some of the more radical Pharisees, the Zealots, disagreed. They felt that the Kingdom of God on earth would never be established so long as Rome continued to rule. The Zealots realized that the much-hoped-for Messiah would never be able to rule as the Jewish king unless he was acceptable to the Romans, for they alone had the power to select the king of the Jews. The Romans, therefore, were blocking the path to the ideal commonwealth. They had to be fought tooth and nail, or else the Jews would never achieve the aims of their religion.

Another group of Jews, the Essenes, had a different concept of the Messiah. They were people full of despair; they regarded the world as a place full of evil; full of immorality, impurity, and poverty. They saw no hope on the horizon. Rome seemed too powerful ever to be overcome; and even if it should be defeated, the Jewish rulers, like Herod, would turn Palestine into a heathen land. The Essenes therefore gave up hope that good would ever come into this world and centered their thoughts on "the world to come." There, they believed, people would be compensated for their suffering on earth. To them, this was the kind of kingdom the Messiah would usher in when he would come to earth on clouds of glory—the Kingdom of Heaven.

They withdrew themselves into little colonies, to live lives of work, abstinence, and holiness. They gave up all their possessions to the common treasury of the brotherhood and waited for the miraculous coming of the Messiah, devoting themselves to pure thoughts and pious acts.

The emphasis of the Essenes upon a life after death was paralleled in non-Jewish communities as well. For Gentiles, too, were suffering from the oppression of Rome. Many Gentiles, particularly the poor and dispossessed, were also seeking some sign of hope. They had no thoughts of a Messiah, for that was part of Jewish tradition, not of theirs. Instead of brotherhoods like the Essenes, despairing Gentiles organized sects with secret rituals, usually involving a solemn blood sacrifice in which all the devotees participated. The idea behind these MYSTERY RELIGIONS was the belief that the secret rites performed would assure those who took part in them the happiness they missed on earth, in a life after death; that the sacred blood of their sacrifices would in some mysterious way bring them "salvation." They, too, had given up hope of relief from suffering during their lifetime.

During the frequent periods of depression under Greek and Roman rule, many ideas concerning a Day of Judgment and life after death had begun to circulate in the Jewish community. Jewish writers wrote many books describing the "coming of the Day of the Lord," when the good would be rewarded for their suffering on earth. They did not sign their names to these books; instead they credited them to Abraham, Enoch, Moses, Solomon, Isaiah, and other respected leaders of ancient times, in order to make the new ideas seem part of Jewish tradition. The poor among the Jews in particular, but others as well, found solace and hope in these books.

So deeply did Jews yearn for a deliverer that, when a Jew by the name of Theudas declared himself to be the Messiah, and offered to prove it by having God cause the River Jordan to become dry, many believed him. He brought them to the banks of the river; but no miracle came. The troops of Rome, however, did come; many Jews were killed, and the Romans cut off Theudas' head and displayed it in Jerusalem as a warning to Jews that only Rome could decide who was to rule them.

Many also responded to the call of a Jew who has come to be known as John the Baptist. He was probably a member of some Essene colony, and used to bathe daily in the Jordan, performing a rite of purification to wash away his sins. John went about dressed as the Prophet Elijah of ancient Hebrew days, wearing a cloak of goatskin and rough sandals, and carrying a staff. There was a legend long current among Jews that Elijah would announce the coming of the Messiah. John identified himself with Elijah and called upon the Jews to prepare themselves for the imminent arrival of the Messiah. He called upon them to repent, to show their desire to live the good life by taking the ceremonial bath with him in the waters of the Jordan. And many Jews did.

John, too, was disposed of. Not only had he publicly

criticized Herod Antipas, the ruler, for his immoral behavior, but John's proclamation that the day of the Messiah
was at hand was causing considerable excitement among
the Jews. Herod was not only angry, he was also worried,
since the Romans, by whose grace he ruled, regarded all
talk about Messiahs as treason. He therefore arrested John
and had his head cut off.

And in the days when Pontius Pilate was the Roman
governor of Palestine, another Jew claimed that he was the
Messiah. He was Joshua (or Jeshua), from the district of
Galilee, better known by the Greek form of his name,
Jesus. A follower of the learned rabbis, he listened to their
discussions in the synagogue schools and accepted many of
the religious ideas of the Pharisees. He was also impressed
by John the Baptist's assurance that the day of the Messiah
was at hand.

He was the son of a carpenter, and spent much of his
time with workers, and with social and economic outcasts.
Many Jews were worried because, for many reasons, they
could not observe all the rites of purification and dietary
laws that Judaism contained. To these Jesus brought con-
solation by assuring them that they were upstanding members of the Jewish fold so long as they sincerely tried to
observe as many of the laws as they could. He brought
them the message of the Pharisaic rabbis, that the Torah
aimed to prepare Jews for the good life, and that the main
requirement of the religion was that people show one another mercy, love, and kindness.

He was doing what other Jewish teachers (rabbis) of his
time were occupied with, explaining the meaning of the
religion to the people. Many rabbis had already become

famous for their interpretations of the religion. In the generation before Jesus, Rabbi Hillel had built up an important school based on a liberal interpretation of Judaism, his main teaching being that people should not do to others what they would not have others do to them. A contemporary of Hillel, Rabbi Shammai, on the other hand, attracted many Jews to his school, where Judaism was interpreted in stricter, more legalistic terms. The aspect of the Jewish faith that Jesus emphasized was its spirit of love and compassion, an approach more in keeping with the outlook of Hillel. Jesus, working among the poor, attracted many of the unlearned to him, who regarded him as a man of exceptional spiritual power.

Jesus and some of his followers came one spring to Jerusalem, to celebrate, with tens of thousands of other pilgrims, the great festival of Pesach, or Passover, in the holy city. This is the festival to commemorate the liberation of the Hebrews from Egyptian slavery, and in those days Jews from all over pilgrimaged to Jerusalem for the special services at the Temple. On the way, Jesus intimated to his closest disciples that he was the promised Messiah. The word spread among other Jews who were making the pilgrimage to Jerusalem. They were eager to see him; and by the time he had come to the gates of the city, large numbers were ready to hail him.

His arrival was of interest to the Romans as well, for a good many Jews were showing him unmistakable respect and deference. The Romans always kept Jerusalem under strict watch during the festival periods, since as many as a million Jews came to the city at those times to offer sacrifices at the Temple. It would be dangerous for the

Romans if a rebellion were touched off at such a time, so they stationed men everywhere to keep an eye on things. Even the governor, Pontius Pilate, was on hand, in case any trouble should break out.

Like the other Jews, Jesus made his way to the Temple. In the court of the Temple he saw people selling cattle and doves for use as sacrifices; there were also tables at which men changed the money brought from distant lands into Palestinian currency, for which service they charged a fee. To Jesus, brought up on Pharisaic teachings, such business, conducted within the very precincts of the Temple, was unholy and desecrating. He became angry at the sight of it and denounced the Sadducees and priests for turning the Temple into a commercial enterprise. He became so aroused that he rushed over to the money-changers and overturned their tables, scattering their coins all over. Then he and his followers chased them out of the Temple court.

Jesus became even more popular as a result of this forthright action. Not only was it accepted as the act of a holy man, but many Jews interpreted it as defiance of Roman rule as well. The rumor that he was the Messiah spread. An air of expectancy hung over Jerusalem. Many Jews waited for something to happen.

That night, when Jerusalem was asleep, the Romans came to the house in the workers' quarter where Jesus and his disciples had celebrated the Seder—the traditional Passover feast—and arrested him. When he admitted that he had claimed to be the Messiah, Pontius Pilate ordered him executed immediately as a traitor to Rome, even though it was a Jewish Holy Day.

But Pilate had no sympathy for Jewish religious sensibility. When he had been appointed Procurator over Palestine in the year A.D. 25, he had been advised to curb Jewish "fanaticism." He had therefore moved his headquarters from Caesarea, a pagan city, to Jerusalem. It mattered little to him that the eagle of the emperor, which adorned the standards and shields of the Roman soldiers, was an abomination to the Jews of the holy city. Pilate withdrew the soldiers only after an insistent demonstration by the Jews, and the payment of a bribe. Another time, the Jews had protested against Pilate's highhanded methods, when he helped himself to some of the Temple treasury, money held sacred by the Jews since it was for the support of the Temple and the priesthood. They had even been forced to complain to Emperor Tiberius when Pilate insisted on hanging Roman shields in his palace in the city, an unnecessary affront to Jewish religious feeling.

After Jesus had been executed, Pilate, in accordance with Roman custom, ordered a placard hung on the cross, stating the crime for which Jesus was executed, as a warning to others. The sign read, "Jesus of Nazareth, King of the Jews." To Pilate, anyone who claimed to be the Messiah— to him that meant only King of the Jews—was thereby committing treason to Rome.

To many Jews the crucifixion of Jesus was just another incident, in a long chain of incidents, attesting to Roman cruelty and ruthlessness. Other leaders had gone down in blood before him. To other Jews, however, to the dispossessed and downtrodden especially, who had come to love Jesus, his execution was nothing short of a catastrophe. They firmly believed that he had been the Messiah, and they hoped and prayed that he would some day return to bring the peace and joy of Judgment Day to the world.

Jews who held such beliefs organized themselves into a society which came to be known by later generations as the Judaeo-Christians (that is, *Jews* who accepted Jesus as the *Christos*—the Greek word for the Hebrew *Moshiach*, which means "anointed" as king). They preached among the Jews the second coming of Jesus, trying to persuade them of the truth of their beliefs. This was quite within the Jewish tradition of religious discussion, in which Pharisees, Essenes, and other Jewish groups were always engaged. The Judaeo-Christians were viewed by the leaders of the Jews as simply another sect within Judaism. The Judaeo-Christians did not go outside the Jewish community to win adherents; only a Jew, they said, only one who accepted the laws of the Torah, could become a Judaeo-Christian.

Christianity might never have developed into a separate and distinct religion had it not been for a remarkable man by the name of Saul, a Jew born in the city of Tarsus, an impressionable person, possessed of a lively imagination. One day, while on a journey to Damascus, Paul (he is better known by his Greek name) was overcome by a vision in which he was called upon to accept Jesus as the Messiah. Paul thereupon became a Judaeo-Christian, but he differed from them in certain fundamental matters of belief, and in his attitude toward the Torah.

To Paul, Jesus was not only the promised Messiah but the immaculately conceived Son of God, who had come to earth to save mankind. Paul believed that everybody came into the world with a sinful nature and had to be "saved" during his lifetime from his evil spirit. To be assured of salvation, a person had to accept Jesus as the Lord, the Saviour who had come to earth to "save" him for the world to come.

Paul believed that Jesus had brought a new revelation from God to supersede the Torah, God's ancient revelation to Moses. The Kingdom of God would be attained *not* through the fulfillment of the laws and observances of the Torah, but through faith in Jesus and acceptance of him as the Son of God.

Paul preached his views in the synagogues in Syria and Asia Minor. There was a period in the synagogue services when any worshiper was invited to read selections from the Torah, and to give an explanation of the section read. Paul eagerly mounted the platform, whenever he got the opportunity, to read specially chosen passages which he then expounded according to the beliefs he held. He argued against the need of circumcision, favoring baptism instead. He urged the dropping of most of the dietary laws and also opposed strict observance of the Sabbath.

He caused many disputes in the synagogues, particularly when he attacked these sacred and traditional Jewish practices. Since most Jews had not accepted Jesus as the promised Messiah, bitter argument frequently ensued. On some occasions Paul was forcibly ejected from the synagogue so the services could continue. Sometimes Jews became so outraged by his strange doctrines that they laid hands on him and beat him in protest.

When the Judaeo-Christian society in Palestine, led by James, a brother of Jesus, and others who had been closest to Jesus, learned what Paul was preaching in their name to Jews and Gentiles alike, they were disturbed. For the

Judaeo-Christians believed in Jesus as the Messiah, but not that he was the Son of God. They believed in circumcision, and observed the Sabbath and the dietary laws. They believed that salvation would come to *all* men who lived according to the Torah. To them, salvation—the Kingdom of God—meant the establishment of the perfect society on this earth, as all Jews believed. Paul's doctrine of individual salvation in heaven, based on faith in Jesus as the Saviour and Son of God who had died for this purpose, was completely foreign to them, and offensive too. They therefore recalled him to Palestine, to protest against his non-Jewish teaching.

After this reprimand, Paul returned to Antioch and Syria. His success among the Jews of those areas had been very limited; but when he preached among Gentiles he made many converts, whom he organized into a number of congregations. So successful was he that the Judaeo-Christians decided to let Paul continue his work among Gentiles on his own terms: that the laws of the Jewish Torah need not be observed by his Gentile converts. The Judaeo-Christians would meanwhile take over all proselytizing among Jews.

To the Gentiles, Paul's ideas were not so strange as they seemed to Jews. They, more readily than Jews, accepted the doctrine of the Immaculate Conception, since in their own myths and legends their gods had begotten children of human beings. They could also accept the concept of salvation through Jesus who had shed his blood for them, since their mystery religions were based on a blood sacrifice, a mystic rite that assured them of bliss in the world to come. Under Paul this contact-with-the-sacrifice idea was blended with the traditional Jewish custom of serving bread and wine, over which a blessing was said, after certain synagogue services. Paul transformed this into a solemn ceremony of identification with Jesus, by declaring that the worshipers, instead of partaking of bread and wine, were partaking in fact of the body and blood of Jesus. This ceremony was later developed into the Christian sacrament of communion.

Paul considered his congregations as representative of true Judaism, of the new revelation which he believed had replaced the Torah. When the Scriptures were read at their services, they were interpreted according to the doctrines enunciated by Paul. Nevertheless, the converted Gentiles still considered themselves as Jews.

But Paul himself was resentful against the Jews because they rejected his Messiah, and also because they would not heed him when he preached his un-Jewish doctrines in the synagogues. His teaching and writings often betrayed this anger. There was also considerable religious rivalry between Paul's followers and the Jews, since both were attempting to convert the Gentiles. The Jews had also been quite successful in their efforts to win converts; even in Rome itself there were Gentile observers of the Sabbath and the dietary laws.

The animosity against the Jews, born of religious rivalry and the need to differentiate between Paul's religious doctrines and the Jewish faith, led Christian leaders to make outright attacks upon the Jews and Judaism to keep Gentiles from entering the Jewish fold. The antagonism grew to such a pitch that Christian religious tracts, such as the "Gospel according to John" which was written about two generations after Jesus, placed the entire blame for the crucifixion of Jesus upon the Jews. Nevertheless, the Romans considered the "Christian" congregations as part of the Jewish community, and their members as Jews.

During this period, and on into the A.D. 60's, the hatred of the Jews against their Roman rulers deepened. The evil symbol of Rome was ever present, in the person of the greedy and corrupt Procurators who ruled over Palestine. One of the worst of these was Florus, who was appointed to Judea in the year A.D. 64.

Florus was a real plunderer; the high taxes he exacted not being sufficient for his greed, he ordered his troops to confiscate money from the Temple treasury. A number of Jews, disgusted with this money-mad official, passed around a basket among the crowd that was watching the troops at their evil work. Each Jew dropped in a small coin and the basket was then given to the leader of the Roman detachment to be presented to Florus. They didn't know he was so poor, said the Jews, so they had taken up this collection for him.

Florus was infuriated at this, and in revenge sent some more soldiers to the city to teach the flippant Jews a lesson. The Jews suffered many casualties; there was much looting, and a few Jews were crucified to atone for the "insult" to the emperor's representative.

He also ordered the Jews to give a proper reception to a special company of Roman soldiers that he was sending to Jerusalem, as a sign of their respect for the emperor. This was just too much for the Zealots and others among the Jews, since it meant hailing the eagle of the emperor, equal in their eyes to acknowledging him as God. The Zealots gave the soldiers a special reception—a hail of stones, thrown in anger. It was the incident that started a bloody war for independence.

Before the Jews could fight Rome as a united people, some internal problems had to be settled. The Sadducees, comprising the priests, wealthy merchants, and plantation owners, were not eager to fight; they had prospered under Roman rule. Some of the Pharisees were not so eager, either; they feared that Rome would not only put down the rebellion but would also destroy the religion, something they valued more than political independence. The Zealots could not stop to talk things over—they simply took the leadership into their own hands and organized the rebellion. Many Pharisees left Jerusalem for other areas of Palestine, where they hastened to establish new synagogue schools to insure the continuation of the faith. Some Sadducees, like the Tories in the American Revolution, went over to the enemy or aided them from within.

To the Romans the war with the Jews was no trifling revolt. The Jews were zealous fighters, and Emperor Nero dispatched his leading general, Vespasian, to Palestine. In the midst of the war, Vespasian was recalled to Rome to become the new emperor, and his son Titus continued the campaign. He laid siege to Jerusalem and started to batter down the walls of the city. The Zealots were not the surrendering kind, however. When the Romans finally made a breach in the walls, they found the Jews had built a second, inner wall in the city. But the brave and courageous Jews were no match for the Romans and their advanced machines of war. After a year of siege, the Romans finally broke through in A.D. 70 on the ninth day of the Hebrew

month of Ab—*Tishah b'Ab*—the anniversary of Nebuchadnezzar's destruction of the Temple in 586 B.C.

The Temple was destroyed and its defenders slaughtered.
The Romans took many of the surviving Jews of Jerusalem
as slaves, and some of them were brought to Rome for a
victory parade. The triumph over the Jews was so significant to Vespasian that he had a special monument erected,
the Arch of Titus—which still stands in Rome—on which
the events of the Jewish war were depicted.

In 586 B.C., when the Babylonians destroyed the Temple,
the Jewish people and their religion were in grave danger
of extinction. But in A.D. 70 the religion was not in such
jeopardy, for by that time many Jewish communities outside of Palestine had become established. There was a large,
thriving community in Babylon, over six hundred years old.
In Egypt, particularly in the city of Alexandria, there were
a great many Jews, as there were also in Rome and other
parts of the empire. A definite culture pattern based on the
religion had also developed among Jews. Jews everywhere
believed in the moral perfection of God and in the Prophetic ideal of brotherhood. They celebrated the same festivals, observed the same dietary laws, and performed the
same ceremonies in their homes and synagogues wherever
they dwelt. They were also devoted to study and learning,
a love the Pharisees had inculcated among the Jews.

Jews had even been able to win many converts as a
result of their proselytizing. Great Roman writers like
Horace, Juvenal, and Cicero had felt called upon to raise
their voices in warning against the increasing spread of
Judaism. They feared that Roman religious practices, which
were also political in nature, would be displaced by Judaism.

They therefore tried to ridicule and discredit Jews and Judaism.

The problem that did confront the Jews after A.D. 70 was how to observe their religion now that the Temple, the accepted center of Judaism, had been destroyed. This question was finally settled by Johanan ben Zakkai, who had established a community of scholars and an academy in the Palestinian city of Jabneh during the War for Independence.

Johanan made the synagogue once and for all the center of Jewish life. New rituals were introduced into the synagogue services to parallel those that had been used in the Temple. New prayers were written; for Johanan's dictum was that "prayer replaces the sacrifices, and deeds of loving kindness, the burnt offerings." Synagogue services were held at the very hours that sacrifices had formerly been performed at the Temple. From Jabneh these and other innovations spread to the other Jewish communities until, in time, regularity in worship was established in all of them, a form of worship that did not depend on the existence of a temple or a priesthood.

Rituals and prayers, observances and ceremonials were only part of the religion. There were also beliefs and doctrines that had gained currency among the Jews over the centuries. These too had to be regularized so that people would know what was truly Jewish. There was confusion in the Jewish community since Judaeo-Christians and other Jewish sects held conflicting views as to the meaning of the religion. There were so many books circulating among Jews that even the rabbis in the academies themselves were not quite sure which of them were to be studied, which of them were worthy of being called sacred.

Johanan therefore called an assembly of rabbis at Jabneh about the year A.D. 90. All the books were studied and their degree of holiness debated. The conference accepted the Torah as sacred without question, since it was considered to be the direct word of God; the books of the Prophets were also declared sacred, because the Prophets' messages were regarded as *inspired* by God; and the other books of what is now the Hebrew Bible—the Old Testament—were included because great heroes of the past were believed to have written these books, or because they dwelt on these heroes and their achievements.

Many books written during the Greek and Roman period were excluded from the Bible. Most of these books dealt mainly with the problems of life after death and other mystical subjects. Others contained ideas somewhat foreign to the teaching and spirit of Judaism. They conflicted with the principle of "Torah is Life," that the Torah is a guide for life in *this* world. Since they did not meet this test, being concerned more with life in "the world to come," they were declared non-Jewish, and the reading of them was frowned upon and discouraged. For some time, however, Jews kept them hidden and read them in private. Certain of these books came to be known as the "Apocrypha," the Greek translation of the Hebrew word *genuzah* (hidden).

It was precisely in these books of the Apocrypha, and in other forbidden books, that the congregations that followed Paul's teaching found passages which they interpreted as proving their points about Jesus as the promised Messiah and about the new doctrines. When the Catholic Church made up its own collection of Sacred Scriptures, more than two hundred years after Johanan's assembly, it included many of these very books that the Jews had excluded from their Bible. But for their inclusion in the Christian sacred writings these books might have been lost to mankind, altogether.

Although Jerusalem was a wasteland, Johanan ben Zakkai's work at Jabneh maintained for Palestine its place of leadership in Jewish life. The Jews of Palestine never gave up hope that Jerusalem would be rebuilt, and when Hadrian, the Roman emperor, made a tour of the eastern part of his empire in the year 130, a Jewish delegation asked him, when he visited Palestine, to rebuild Jerusalem. Hadrian thought it a good idea, but he decided to rebuild it as a completely heathen city, dedicated to the worship of the Roman god, Jupiter.

This was a deep affront to the Jews, and the smoldering hatred against Rome was rekindled. Extensive preparation for a new revolt was made, led by the respected and wealthy Rabbi Akiba, who selected Simon Bar Kochba to lead the rebellion. To get the maximum support from the Jewish communities, Akiba announced that Bar Kochba was the promised Messiah. The Christians of Palestine dissociated themselves from the Jewish rebellion because they recognized only Jesus as the Messiah, but practically all the Jews rallied to Bar Kochba's standard.

The revolt broke out in 132 and the Jews inflicted great losses upon the Romans. Hadrian had to call in from Europe his best generals and finest soldiers. Exasperated, Hadrian declared all-out war against Judaism, as well as against the Jewish people. He issued edicts against all phases of the Jewish religion, forbidding the teaching of the Torah and

Under the Roman Eagle

the observance of the Sabbath, ordering all schools, synagogues, and Jewish courts closed. He also forbade circumcision and decreed death for all who violated his edicts.

The Christian congregations, in order to make certain that the bans would not include them, declared themselves outside the fold of Judaism. Thus they made the break with the Jewish community complete. They were now a separate body—*Christians*—following a distinct religion of their own.

The violent war came to an end in 135. It had cost the Romans heavily; it hit the Jews even harder. More than half a million Jews were killed or captured during the fighting; countless others suffered heavy losses in property, and various community institutions were destroyed. Many of the leading scholars, who had defied Hadrian and had continued to teach, were liquidated; others fled to the freer air of Babylon and other communities outside the Roman Empire.

Hadrian did build his Roman city, Aelia Capitolina, on the site of Jerusalem. Jews were excluded, but Christians, who were now acknowledged as a Gentile sect, were permitted to settle there.

In the reign of Antoninus Pius, 138–161, the harsh decrees against Judaism were abolished. Some Jews returned to Palestine, and some of the schools and community institutions were rebuilt. But Palestine was no longer the shining citadel of the Jewish faith. Its population had shrunk, and its economic life had become shattered as a result of the war. The people could no longer support the great academies the Pharisees had established, and only a few small ones remained.

In the face of the disintegration of the Palestinian community, some of the scholars felt it necessary to take steps to preserve the Oral Law—the interpretations of the Torah that the Palestinian rabbis had been making. These laws, while they were accepted as religious commandments, had not been written down, since they were regarded as man-made laws, distinct from the written Torah, the Law as revealed by God. In the days when the Palestinian academies were filled with students, the Oral Law had been kept alive as students of each generation memorized them. But now, with fewer students, the vast number of oral decisions was in danger of being lost or forgotten. So scholars began to codify the laws, to make it easier to memorize them.

The codification of the Oral Law was completed about the year 200 by Judah Hanasi, the president of the Palestinian Sanhedrin. His compilation, known as the Mishnah, arranged all the decisions systematically, according to their subject matter. The Mishnah was not regarded as the final word in the religion; Judah made it clear that succeeding generations of scholars could continue to interpret the Law to fit whatever new conditions might arise.

In the years following the completion of the Mishnah, the Palestinian schools declined further; the community was weak and spent and students were no longer drawn to them. They gravitated toward those Jewish settlements where conditions were more stable economically and therefore more conducive to learning and study, especially to the Babylonian area of the Persian Empire. Leadership in Jewish life shifted to the Persian Jewish community, from which Ezra and Nehemiah had come, centuries before, to help establish the Jewish commonwealth in Palestine.

CHAPTER NINE

The Expanding Jewish Horizon

A LARGE Jewish population had existed in Babylon ever since 586 B.C. By the year A.D. 200 the Jews of that area had become an integral part of the Persian Empire; in language, dress, and occupations, in all aspects of life except religion, they were like their neighbors.

Farming was their main occupation; some Jews engaged in cattle and sheep raising and some in wine culture. There were also many Jewish artisans and merchants in the cities, some of whom took part in foreign trade with India and China to the east, and Syria and Palestine to the west.

The Persian rulers recognized the Jews as a people within the empire, a separate group with the right of self-government. This did not mean that Jews were excluded from the political life of the empire; in fact, many Jews rose to high position in the Persian government, and Jews themselves felt that Persia was their native land. While Jews recognized Persian law as supreme, they nevertheless were given the special privilege of organizing their communities according to their own religious laws.

Each Jewish community had its council to collect and distribute charity, to maintain order, and to regulate commercial life. The council was also in charge of the synagogue, the town hall, the cemetery, and the *Bet Hamidrash* (the Academy). Over all the communities presided the Exilarch (the Head of the Exile), whom the Persian government recognized as the civil head of all the Jews. He was the link between the Jews and the Persian government, and was charged by them with the task of collecting the taxes levied by the Persian government.

In the tradition of the Pharisees, Persian Jews regarded education as a prime necessity of the religion. In fact, a Jew's social standing was determined by the quality and extent of his knowledge of the Torah and the Oral Law, more than by his wealth or family connections. Nor was education limited to the study of Jewish law, ethics, and tradition; many Jews also studied Persian science: astronomy, mathematics, and medicine.

Life in Persia, compared to Palestine under the claws of the Roman eagle, was very favorable for Jewish study; and many Jewish academies did flourish, especially those at Nehardea and Sura, which attracted many students from near and far.

The teachers and students of Nehardea and Sura studied and memorized the Palestinian Mishnah, and applied its decisions to the everyday life of the people, often amending the laws to suit the conditions of life in Persia. From time to time, they developed new laws altogether. These were in turn memorized and brought into future discussions. So famous did these academies become that Jews in various parts of the world turned to the Persian rabbis rather than to those of Palestine for religious guidance.

With the years a very great number of decisions enlarging upon the Mishnah accumulated. In order to make known the new religious rules, the academies began to convene special assemblies, known as Kallahs. These gatherings were held twice a year (before Passover and Rosh Hashanah, the Jewish New Year), and as many as twelve thousand representatives of local and distant communities attended them. At the conclusion of the Kallahs they returned to their own communities to report, and to put into effect, the new decisions. In this way, the Persian academies helped to develop a degree of uniformity in religious practice among Jews wherever they lived.

Life in Persia was not all serene. Occasionally, Jewish communal life was disrupted. Most Persians were of the Zoroastrian faith, based on the teachings of Zoroaster, which they regarded as superior to all other religions. When the Zoroastrian priests in A.D. 226, gained control over the Persian ruler, they began to persecute the non-Zoroastrian population, including the Jews. They restricted Jewish study and forbade a number of religious observances. However, they did not stay in power long enough to destroy Jewish life completely. Then in the year 250, the Romans invaded Persia; during this war, the Nehardea settlement, where the famous academy was situated, was destroyed. After the Jews had helped drive the Romans out of the country, they built a new academy in the town of Pumbeditha, which soon began to vie for leadership with the school at Sura.

After two centuries of calm and peace, a fanatical sect of Persians again came into power. They enforced many decrees against Jews, Christians, and others. The Jewish academies and Kallahs were closed and many of their teachers were executed. After about twenty years, conditions once again returned to normal and the Jews began to rebuild their communal life.

They decided then to put the Oral Law into writing. There was by now such an accumulation of opinions and decisions that it taxed even the most prodigious of memorizers. Furthermore, the Persians had killed off quite a number of Jewish scholars. The Mishnah and all the opinions and decisions resulting from three hundred years of discussion of it were put together into one monumental work which was completed about the year A.D. 500, called the Babylonian Talmud.

The Talmud was sacred to the Jews. The hundreds of scholars and teachers who had contributed to it over the centuries had poured into it their deep sense of identification with God, the feeling that had been instituted among Jews by Moses and reintensified by the Prophets. Through their interpretations of the Torah, the rabbis of old had tried to keep alive the principles of the ancient covenant by applying them to every activity of life. For the Jews the Talmud became the new "constitution." It was studied in all Jewish communities, and its laws and dicta were applied, directly or in modified form, to their way of life. It thus bound the geographically separated Jews more closely together in thought and action.

The Jews who lived in lands under the control of the Roman Empire, meanwhile, became the victims of persecu-

tion, too, along with others who did not accept the doctrines of the Roman Catholic Church, which had become
the dominant religion of the empire. Some Christian preachers made animosity toward Judaism their major theme. By
A.D. 306, when leaders of the Church held a conference at
Elvira, Spain, the hostility was given practical expression
when they forbade Christians to eat with Jews, and condemned a custom that had developed in Spain of having
rabbis bless the fields of Christian farmers.

This antagonistic attitude had been made completely
official by the Council of Nicaea in the year 325. The
bishops of the Church met at Nicaea to establish a uniform
creed for Christianity, since many conflicting doctrines had
been preached in its name in the course of its nearly three
hundred years of existence. The "Nicene Creed" which
they adopted recognized Jesus as the Lord, and the Bishop
of Rome as the Pope or head of the Church, the "vicar of
Christ on earth."

It was at this council that the Christian Bible was adopted
officially. The bishops altered the sequence of the books of
the Jewish Bible, as they had been arranged at Jabneh
more than two hundred years earlier; to these they added
the Apocrypha, to form the Christian version of the Old
Testament. This arrangement made it seem that all of Jewish history had been but the preparation for the coming of
Jesus and the new revelation, Christianity.

The teachings of Christianity itself were embodied in the
writings the council selected for the New Testament. Many
of these books contained the attacks upon Jews and Judaism
that had stemmed from the religious competition between
the two faiths. The council made clear the official position

of the Church toward Jews in a simple and devastating manner: Christians were "to have nothing in common with the murderers of the Lord."

From 325 on, therefore, the position of the Jews in the Roman Empire became precarious. From the time of Emperor Antoninus Pius the Jews had had certain civil and religious rights, for Judaism had been recognized by Roman law as a legal religion. But, as the influence of the Church upon the Roman rulers became stronger, the protection of Roman law was gradually taken from the Jews. Instead of rights, they now had restrictions placed on their lives and activities. Jewish proselytizing was forbidden; they were deprived of the right to replace or renovate old synagogues; various occupations were closed to them; and they were prevented from holding any government or other position that would put them in authority over Christians.

The spread of Christianity had a profound effect on the Jews who lived in lands under the control of the Roman Empire. And in the 600's, in Arabia, there arose a new religion, Mohammedanism, which also influenced strongly the development of the Jews.

In Arabia, far from the Persian academies, lived a large number of Jews who practiced their religion undisturbed, since Arabia had no single faith to which the Arabians thirsted to convert all of mankind. In fact, the Arabs respected the Jewish reverence for the Torah, and called the Jews "the people of the book."

A moody camel driver from Mecca, an Arab by the name of Mohammed, was deeply impressed by the belief of the Jews in a Universal God, and by their personal morality. On his travels he had become acquainted with Jewish and

Christian customs, their modes of worship, lore, and legends. He was filled with a desire to improve the life of his people. It seemed to him that they could profit from Jewish and Christian ideas, for the backwardness of the Arabs and their low moral values saddened him.

Increasingly, as he thought of these matters, he was thrown into deep trances. When he came out of them he announced that he had been visited by an angel of God who had revealed new truths to him. The revelations he uttered were written down into a book, the Koran, which later became the Bible of his new religion. Mohammed declared himself to be *the* Prophet of God (Allah, in Arabic), above Moses and Jesus, both of whom he recognized as great, but less important, spokesmen of God. The Koran, which he claimed was God's latest revelation, was therefore in his eyes greater than the Jewish and Christian Bibles.

He expected the Jews of Arabia to become converted to his new religion, since he not only believed in circumcision and dietary laws, used no priests as mediators between man and God, and directed his prayers toward Jerusalem, which he regarded as a Holy City, but also found a tie of blood in the Biblical hint that both Arabs and Jews were descended from Abraham. But the Arabian Jews did not flock to him: they did not believe Mohammed to be greater than Moses, and they felt that God had revealed Himself to mankind for all time in the Torah.

Nor did many Arabs flock to him, for he attacked their pagan practices and insisted that they substitute prayers for traditional sacrifices. Nor were they ready to accept the Jewish and Christian ethical and moral principles he urged upon them. He made many enemies in Mecca, and in 622 he had to flee for his life to the city of Medina.

It was an angry Mohammed who came to Medina with his faithful disciples; angry at the Arabs in Mecca who had plotted against him, and aroused at the Jews who had spurned him. In the course of two years in Medina, however, he won so many converts among the Arabs of that city, that he was able to raise a large army. Then, in 624 he attacked and defeated the Meccans. He converted the conquered Arabs of Mecca to his new religion; his fame increased and his religion began to spread.

He lashed out against the Jewish tribes, confiscating their property, enslaving them, and putting to the sword many who refused to adopt Islam (the religion of the Mohammedans). While he forced Arabs, Jews, and Christians to become converted, there were large numbers of Arabs, and many Jews and Christians, who voluntarily accepted the new faith. By 632, the year of his death, he had conquered all of Arabia.

Meanwhile, Mohammed had added new revelations to the Koran which changed certain aspects of his religion. Mecca had become the Holy City to which all prayers were to be directed, and he had commanded the faithful to make annual religious pilgrimages to it. He had dropped the fast of the Jewish Day of Atonement and substituted for it the Ramadhan, a month during which the faithful were to fast from sunrise to sunset. And he had established Friday as the Mohammedan Sabbath (the Jews had Saturday, the Christians Sunday).

The land in Arabia and Mesopotamia, where the Mohammedans were entrenched, had been exhausted by centuries of unscientific farming. The Moslems were urged by their leaders, in the name of Allah, to conquer new homes for themselves and their religion. This they set out to do with tenacity and fierceness, for Mohammed had promised eternal bliss in a heavenly paradise for all who, for the glory of Allah, died on the battlefield. In 635 they conquered Palestine, the following year Persia, and in 640 they overran Egypt. The Arab armies spilled over into North Africa, went clear across the continent to Morocco. And then, in the year 711, they crossed the Strait of Gibraltar, conquering Spain after four years. From there they penetrated northeastward into France, but were finally driven back to Spain in 732.

The Arabs did not come for spoil and plunder. They settled down to live in the conquered territories and to convert the people to Islam. In the early years of the religion, the Mohammedan leaders, the caliphs, persecuted all nonbelievers. They were forbidden to criticize either Mohammed or the Koran; they were not to prevent anyone from becoming converted to Islam; and they were not allowed to build new houses of worship, although they were permitted to repair old ones. Special taxes were levied on nonbelievers, who were compelled to wear something special to distinguish them from Moslems, since Jews and Christians in Moslem lands dressed, spoke, and looked like their neighbors. There were many other restrictions, but soon after the Mohammedan Empire was firmly established, the caliphs did not bother to enforce these regulations. Jews and Christians even rose to high positions under the caliphs.

The growing tolerance of the Mohammedan rulers made Jewish life more secure. The Jews of Palestine were given greater freedom, being permitted to settle anywhere in the country, even in Jerusalem. Their interest in learning revived and they built an academy in the city of Tiberias which became famous in the Jewish world. In Persia they were able to reopen their academies. The Egyptian Jewish community began to grow, attracting Jews from other lands. Wherever the Mohammedans conquered, their mosques and minarets stood out like mileposts to mark their victorious path. Busy synagogues also appeared along the route of march, symbols of a revived Jewish life.

As the Arabs came in contact with the fine old civilizations, they adopted their established skills and occupations, and their scholars mastered the languages and learning of the conquered peoples. The ancient books of the Graeco-Roman world, and of India, were translated into Arabic and studied in the various colleges they established throughout their empire. The Mohammedan scholars achieved a reputation for extensive learning in a period when Europe was, intellectually, in the Dark Ages.

They brought their knowledge, skill and experience—their superior civilization—to Spain. They built up the trade and commerce of that country and introduced their books of learning, their own and what they had found in other lands. Under Mohammedan rule, Spain prospered; it became one of the wealthiest and most cultured lands of the Middle Ages.

For the Jews, who had been living in Spain since early Roman times, this was indeed a welcome change. For they had lived through the troubled days when the barbarian tribe of Vandals, and later the Visigoths, had invaded the country. Those wars had brought the Spanish people, including the Jews, poverty and suffering. Although the Visigoth rulers were Christians, the Jews had suffered no extra hardships because of it. For the Visigoths had not adopted the Nicene Creed; they did not believe in the divinity of Jesus; and they did not recognize the Pope as their spiritual head. The Visigoths had also not adopted the anti-Jewish attitude that had been made official Christian doctrine in 325. In the eyes of the Roman Catholic Church they were not true Christians.

In the year 589, however, Reccared I, the Visigoth king of Spain, in order to strengthen his hold upon the country, became a Roman Catholic. He thus secured the support of the Church in his quarrels with the semi-independent nobles and lords in his country. In return he was required to enforce the decrees of the Church, including the anti-Jewish ones.

After the Mohammedan conquest of Spain in 715, the Jews shared in the prosperity and cultural progress of the country. A steady stream of Mohammedans and Jews from North Africa and from the exhausted regions of the East flowed toward Spain. The Jewish communities grew, and schools were established at Cordoba and other cities.

Contact with Mohemmedan thought and literature produced a new emphasis in Jewish learning and interests. The Mohammedans loved poetry and imaginative writing. Influenced by this aspect of Mohammedan culture, Jews in Palestine, Spain, and elsewhere became interested in poetry and creative literature. Jewish scholars wrote poetic prayers for the synagogue services, many of which were filled with yearning for the restoration of Zion. As these poems gradually found their way into the services of worship in the other Jewish communities, the longing for the restoration of Zion, supplementing the prayers already in the liturgy, became part of the culture pattern of the Jews everywhere. In the eleventh century Solomon ibn Gabirol of Spain wrote religious poetry of such fine quality that some of his hymns are still read, especially in the liturgy for Yom Kippur, the Day of Atonement. Judah Halevi's poems, written in Spain about the same time, are also read today, many of his hymns being sung in synagogues.

In the Persian schools, however, the scholars concentrated all their attention on the laws of the religion, defining and redefining the practices and ceremonies that were obligatory for Jews. They regarded the Talmud as the perfect guide to Jewish living; all that was necessary was to study its laws and to make whatever amendments seemed necessary wherever problems came up.

Yet all about them in the eastern Mohammedan world, Jews were witnessing exciting intellectual activity. The Mohammedan scholars were studying the books of the great Greek philosophers such as Plato and Aristotle; their thinkers were speculating on such problems as the nature of God and the universe, and the meaning and purpose of life itself. Many Jews were intrigued by these discussions, and felt they were important for a true understanding of the world they lived in. To such Jews, the hairsplitting legal debates of the Babylonian Talmudic scholars were like a fog obscuring the ideals of the Prophets and the Torah. They felt that Judaism was being driven into a rut, a dull, burdensome routine of ritual and ceremonial observances.

A restive spirit developed among the Jews in Persia and other eastern Mohammedan lands. Many began to object to the narrow outlook of the Gaonim, the heads of the Babylonian schools, and to reject their interpretations and decisions. One of these objectors was Anan ben David. Besides his opposition to their overemphasis on Talmudic laws, Anan had personal reasons for disliking the Gaonim: they had refused to recommend him for the position of Exilarch, the official head of the Jews in the Persian Empire. His denunciation of the Gaonim became bitter, and they had him imprisoned as a rebel against constituted authority. The Mohammedan caliph, however, released him.

Anan, after the year 760, began to organize his followers into a definite religious community. He discarded the entire Oral Law—the Talmud with all its accumulated laws and observances, including the Rabbinic dietary laws. He dropped the observance of the Hanukkah festival commemorating the Maccabee revolt because it was not mentioned in the Torah. To him, only those ceremonies and commandments expressly stated in the Torah were sacred. Because he insisted that only the Written Law of the Torah was to be observed, his movement became known as *Karaism*, from the Hebrew word *Kara* (to read). Since all other Jews the world over followed the Talmud as their "constitution," Karaism was in effect a different religion.

Under Anan's successors, Benjamin Nahavendi and Daniel Al-Kumisi, Karaism became a formidable movement, attracting large numbers of Jews in Mohammedan lands. To prove that they were right in their attitude toward the Torah, the Karaites studied every word in it, to determine its exact meaning, employing the fine points of grammar and syntax to prove their interpretations. This was a field of knowledge with which most Jewish scholars were unfamiliar so that the Babylonian scholars were quite unable to answer the arguments and interpretations of the Karaites. In some localities the Karaites actually outnumbered the followers of the Talmud, and threatened to disrupt the unity of the Jews altogether.

It wasn't until Saadiah ben Joseph, an Egyptian Jew of great learning, became the Gaon of the Sura Academy in the early 900's that the Karaite schism was ended. Saadiah was a keener Hebrew grammarian than the Karaite leaders themselves. He was able to refute many of their interpretations of various words and passages in the Torah. He pointed out, further, that the position of the Karaites was illogical. They had thrust out the Talmud because it represented interpretations of the Word of God as given in the Torah, but the Karaites themselves had had to make interpretations of the Torah over the years. They had practically developed a "Talmud" of their own. It was not wrong, then, merely to interpret the Torah; the real question was: which explanation was the better, the Karaite, or the Talmudic? He proved to the satisfaction of the vast majority of the Jews that the Rabbis of the Talmud had done a much better job.

But he did not accept the idea that the traditions established by the Talmud were absolutely sacred and unchangeable. It was wrong to stick to interpretations that no longer fitted the changed conditions under which Jews lived. He urged Jews to study the philosophy and books of non-Jews, for they contained many worth-while ideas for the improvement of life. That was the main purpose of religion: to live according to the principles of justice and brotherhood that the Prophets had preached. Nevertheless, if other peoples had ideas and practices that helped to attain those goals, the Jews should know them and take them into consideration when they studied and modified their own religious traditions.

Saadiah did not regard Judaism as the only guide to the good life. He recognized that other religions had contributions to make too, even declaring that God had sent Christianity and Islam into the world for this very purpose. But he felt that Judaism was superior to these faiths, particularly in its ethical and moral philosophy. He wanted Jews in Arabic lands, to most of whom Arabic, and not Hebrew, was their native tongue, to become better acquainted with the beauty and majesty of their Bible, so he translated it into Arabic. He wrote brilliant commentaries to accompany the translation, to explain difficult or obscure passages, and to point out the significant ideas in the Bible.

Saadiah's books pulled the foundation from under the Karaites, and their movement fell apart. This ardent champion of Judaism helped keep many Jews loyal to the religion, who were close to becoming converted to Mohammedanism. He gave the religious leaders a new direction for their future intellectual development: toward the culture of the peoples about them rather than to the confines of the Talmud. He made Judaism a dynamic religion once again, linking it to progress in the world of ideas rather than binding it to the traditions of the past alone; and he instilled among Jews a deep pride in Judaism.

Under Islam, the Jews enjoyed a rich and expanding cultural life. But, unfortunately, the Mohammedan Empire in the East gradually fell apart as a result of more than two hundred years of intermittent wars with Christian rulers of

Europe, especially during the Crusades. Mohammedan culture, as well as Jewish culture, in the old Persian areas of the Mohammedan Empire began to decline. The Mohammedans in Spain, however, carried on with great vigor; and so did the Jews among them.

But life even under Mohammedan rule was not always ideal for non-Moslems. Occasionally, a fanatical caliph would decide to enforce the code against nonbelievers, as was done, for instance, in Spain after 1150. Then Jews, Christians, and other nonbelievers had to become Mohammedans or leave the country. Jewish and Christian schools, synagogues and churches were closed, torn down or converted to Moslem use. Jews and Christians lost their government positions. Many left Spain, but quite a few became converted. Many of the converted Jews, however, secretly continued their traditional Jewish practices, even while outwardly living as Mohammedans.

Such incidents were not very common, nor did they last long; for the Mohammedans, in the main, were tolerant. Jewish life in Spain actually flourished. A new chapter, a very troubled one, however, was about to open for them. As the Mohammedan power in Spain weakened, as Mohammedan power in general disintegrated, more and more Jews came under the rule of Christian kings. And Christian Europe in the Middle Ages was far less tolerant of Jews and Judaism than was the Mohammedan world.

CHAPTER TEN

Under the Cross

THE early Christians had been recruited mainly from the poorer classes. Christian preachers, many with a zeal like that of the ancient Hebrew Prophets, portrayed God as the champion of the common man, as the Jews did, and protested against the increasing wealth and immorality of the ruling classes while hunger and need became the lot of the vast majority of the people.

The early converts to Christianity lived together under a sort of tribal communism, sharing their possessions. The New Testament describes the early Christian communities in the following words: "And all that believed together had all things in common; and they sold all their possessions and goods, and parted them to all men, according as every man had need. . . . And the multitude of them believed they were of one heart and of one soul, and not one of them said aught of the things which he possessed was his own, but they had all things in common."

Such ideas were distasteful to the men of wealth and

power in the Roman Empire. Many emperors, particularly Nero and Diocletian, persecuted the Christians, attacking them as subversive elements. The fact that they refused to observe the pagan custom of sacrificing to the emperor as a god, made it easier to convince Romans that Christians were disloyal. When there was discontent among the people, during periods of famine and unemployment, the rulers blamed the Christians for the people's misfortunes; they stirred up violent attacks upon them to divert the attention of the people from the real causes of their misery by rousing them to work off their dissatisfaction at the expense of the Christians. Decrees were issued making the religion illegal, subjecting all who observed its rites to various punishments. Often Christians were made to fight hungry lions in the amphitheaters for the sport of the Roman populace, who watched the "sporting events" in the Colosseum much as people watch professional prize fights today.

Persecution, however, seemed to help, rather than halt, the spread of Christianity; for it became a completely legal religion by the year 325, when Emperor Constantine, who had become converted to Christianity, abolished all anti-Christian laws. Then the leaders of the Church embarked on a campaign to make the entire Roman Empire Christian, with all its people conforming to the doctrines and rituals of the Church, for it was their belief that only faith in Jesus as the Son of God could "save" mankind; that only through the sacraments of the Church could mankind gain the "keys to the kingdom."

By the year 438 they had induced the emperors, who were by this time Christians, to favor Christianity above all other faiths, and to establish it as the official religion of the empire. The code of laws for the empire, issued in that year by the Emperor Theodosius, declared the doctrines of the Church supreme, to be accepted without question; it also provided for various punishments to be enforced by the state against unbelievers. The clergy of the Church were made a privileged class, exempt from taxes, military service, and other public burdens, and the people were encouraged to give and bequeath lands to the Church for its support.

Through gifts and donations from kings and nobles, the Church became a rich landowning power. The bishops and archbishops became more than spiritual supervisors of the Christians living in the areas assigned to them; they became directors and administrators of large estates worked by slaves and serfs, and supervised the sale of many products from these estates. The Church being now a landlord and also "in business" as it were, the early Apostolic emphasis on sharing the wealth began to disappear.

The emphasis of the Church in this period was on conformity in worship, on having all people observe the sacraments and rituals decreed by the popes and Church councils. But there were many Christians who did not accept all the decisions made by the Council of Nicaea in the year 325. The leaders of the Church branded such Christians as heretics, not to be associated with because they were unbelievers.

Another group that displeased the leaders of the Church was the Jews, for to them Judaism was "the direct antithesis and contradiction of Catholicism." To leading churchmen in Europe in the early Middle Ages, it seemed wrong to have Jews live on equal and friendly terms with Christians, for they deemed Judaism inferior to Christianity and, at the same time, saw it as a rival and competitor of Christianity. Yet, despite the attitude of the officials of the Church, Jews and Christians did live together in social and economic harmony in those days. Christians often attended synagogue services, and visited with Jewish friends on special Jewish feast days; even members of the clergy came to Jewish banquets. Jews were likewise entertained by Christians, by barons as well as commoners. They held friendly discussions, even on such questions as the divinity of Jesus and the Immaculate Conception. Jews and Christians mingled together, as people normally do. Intermarriage was not uncommon between them, with the children frequently being brought up as Jews.

This situation was vexing to the leaders of the Church; they wanted to separate the Christians from the Jews, "to preserve Catholics from such contact with Jews as might cause harm to the purity of their Catholic faith." The Jews knew their Holy Scriptures well, since they were the very basis of the Jewish educational system, while the newly converted Christians had only a spotty knowledge of the Jewish Bible. They were, therefore, not able to answer all the points brought up by Jews when religious discussions came up. Fraternization therefore spelled danger, since it could lead Christians to doubt, rather than accept with unquestioning faith, Christian doctrines and practices.

An example of how greatly aroused the Church was in those early days about the good relations between Jews and Christians, was the series of sermons delivered by Bishop John Chrysostom in 387, in the city of Antioch, utterances bristling with hatred toward the Jews. It was offensive to God, said the bishop, for Christians to associate with Jews, for God hated them, and all Christians should hate them too. They were a people who "sacrificed" their children to the devil. They were the murderers of Jesus.

Since all education, the little there was of it in those days, was in the hands of the Church, the schools were able to indoctrinate many Christians with fear and distrust of the Jews, particularly in those places where no Jews lived. But in those parts of the empire where Jews had lived a long time, it was more difficult to separate Christians from Jews, since they had been on close and friendly terms for so long that it had become part of the social pattern for them to associate with one another. Jews and Christians dressed alike, spoke the same languages, and engaged in the same occupations.

The Church, therefore, exerted its influence upon the emperors and kings to include in their codes of laws restrictions that would weaken the Jewish faith and drive a wedge between Jews and Christians. The new codes decreed that Christians were to cease attending Jewish functions, that intermarriages with Jews constituted a crime punishable by death, and that those Christians who had already intermarried with Jews were to dissolve their marriages on penalty of excommunication.

In the days of Pope Gregory I (590–604), the Church attacked the right of Jews to own Christian slaves. Generally, slaves adopted the religion of their masters; many Christian slaves owned by Jews, therefore, were becoming Jews. Church leaders did not like to see the Jewish population increase; a decree was therefore issued denying Jews the right to own Christian slaves. However, Christians were permitted to own such slaves, in fact, officials of the Church themselves owned many Christian slaves. Another decree forbade Jews to have Christian workers under their authority.

By the time of Pope Gregory I, the Roman Empire had fallen apart and Europe was in a state of turmoil. Barbarian tribes from the East and North had invaded the empire. After much plundering and warfare, the invaders had settled down; but they gave their allegiance to their own chiefs, not to the Roman emperor. The Roman army was so weakened, and the authority of the emperor so limited, that the Roman authorities could no longer enforce the codes of law. With the weakening of the central Roman authority, kings and lords became all powerful in their own domains. They made war on each other to enlarge the lands and estates they ruled. Law and order, which the Roman armies had formerly maintained fairly successfully, broke down.

Trade declined; it became too dangerous to travel, especially with goods or money. With so many lords carving out little empires of their own, merchants had to cross too many frontiers, at which each lord exacted a heavy toll for the right to enter his land. To top it off, the fine Roman-built roads had fallen into disrepair. Many Jews and Christians began to return to the soil, as the only secure way of getting the means for subsistence.

For a number of reasons, however, it became increasingly difficult for the Jews to engage in agriculture in Medieval Europe. Many Church leaders protested against Jewish ownership of land. In the 770's, for instance, Pope Stephen III complained in a letter to the Bishop of Narbonne, France, that "Jews, who revolt against our religion and mock at our customs, have large estates within Christian boundaries, in the cities and outside of them, and Christians till their soil and cultivate their fields." Pope Benedict, in 850, objected to the practice of Christians who hired Jews as foremen on their estates, threatening Christians with excommunication if they continued to employ Jews. The Church appealed to kings and nobles everywhere to prevent Jews from owning land at all.

Naturally, these laws kept large numbers of Jews from establishing themselves on the land. But what finally drove them out of agriculture in Europe altogether was the development of the feudal system. With the disappearance of Roman governmental authority, the small landowner was powerless against the marauding barons and their private armies. To seek protection, the small landowner began to make pacts with neighboring lords. He would vow to serve the lord in various ways, and the lord in turn would vow to protect "his man," which is what the small landowner became, in effect. This type of landholding became the regular custom in Europe. Each lord or bishop had his domain, and the people who lived on that land were his serfs and retainers, who owed him certain feudal dues and services in return for his protection.

Practically every person was somebody's "man"—the serf under the lord, the lord under some more powerful noble, who in turn might be the archbishop's or king's man. The serf's allegiance was to the first lord, not to the king; it was the lord who made the rules for his estate. The Church, being a large landowner, was an important part of the feudal system. Bishops maintained armies like other lords; they were often vassals of kings or powerful nobles, owing them allegiance and military aid. Often, other lords owed them such aid. The bishops were thus involved quite often in the almost continuous feudal wars, and in political activity.

In one sense the Church was in the very center of the feudal system. For the special ceremony by which the serf or vassal became "the man" of the lord was a religious one. All vows between lords and serfs, or kings and vassals, were made "in the name of the Father, the Son, and the Holy Ghost." Jews, therefore, could not take the feudal vow, and therefore could not live on the manorial estates.

The Jews then began to move toward the towns, which were very slowly coming to life again. All activity in the towns was run by the guilds. To be an artisan in a town, or to own a shop, one had to belong to the guild that controlled the particular occupation. But since the guilds were brotherhoods open to Christians only, the Jews could not join. The normal town occupations were therefore closed to them.

To gain a livelihood became a very serious problem to the Jews of Europe. The Church was one of the largest employers of labor, being a far-flung empire with many estates and establishments; its jobs were naturally closed to Jews. Government service was out, since the Church was opposed to having Jews in authority over Christians. The Jews had been forced off the land and denied access to town occupations. Various Church decrees had restricted their work until they were left with the unpopular job of moneylending, which was forbidden to Christians by Church law, and of dealing in second-hand goods.

In the early Middle Ages people held their position in

society by being part of a group or class. They were serfs, knights, lords, members of the clergy, merchants—it was their membership in a particular group that gave people their rights or privileges. But the Jews did not fit into the regular pattern of feudal classes or occupations; they could not obtain protection the way the serfs or vassals did, in return for feudal services. The Jews had to *buy* protection; they had to buy with money the right to live. It was inevitable, therefore, that the emphasis in the Jewish communities of Europe gradually shifted to the accumulation of money and precious articles with which to protect their right to live; for, as Rabbi ben Judah of Mayence wrote, in the tenth century: "Christians cannot be appeased with pleasant words. Only money will satisfy them, and whoever falls into their hands will not go free without payment."

By the end of the tenth century, most of the Jews of Europe, outside of Spain, had been reduced to living precariously as peddlers and moneylenders. There was one advantage the Jews had, however, in not being tied to the land like the serfs. They could move about freely, like the knights and nobles. It was possible for them, therefore, to travel over the countryside with their merchandise, exchanging and selling their second-hand wares. Some of them were also able to engage in international trade.

As time went on trade began to increase, and a good deal of it was carried on by the Jews. In a time when there were few inns and when travel in general was difficult, Jewish merchants were able to travel widely, since there were Jewish communities all over Europe and the East and they could always count on hospitality from their fellow Jews.

People began to regard Jews as desirable elements in the cities, since they could bring trade to whatever section they lived in. They were even offered special inducements to settle in some cities. In 1084, for instance, Bishop Rüdiger Huozmann urged Jews to come to Speyer and promised them many privileges, even to the extent of letting their chief rabbi share with the mayor the right to decide lawsuits. Thus, in the period of the revived interest in trade, many stable Jewish communities were established in various towns and cities of western Europe.

However, a fairly high percentage of what the Jews earned from dealing in money and merchandise was taken from them by high taxes, and by forced payments to lords and kings under threat of expulsion from their domains. Moreover, as trade and commerce became more profitable, and as banking became an increasingly important business, Christians began to enter both occupations in larger numbers. Jewish predominance in trade and banking was short-lived, once Christians became their competitors.

During this period, when the Jews were slowly establishing a meaningful place for themselves in European life, an event occurred which had a shattering effect upon them. It started with an innocent request for help that the Patriarch of the Greek Catholic Church made of Pope Urban II in the year 1095. The Seljuk Turks, a warrior people who had been converted to Islam, had conquered Palestine and other sections of Asia Minor and were threatening Constantinople, the seat of the Greek Catholic Church. Although the Greek Catholics did not recognize the Pope as their head—they were not *Roman* Catholics—the Patriarch hoped that Pope Urban would be interested in fighting the Moslems and liberating Palestine, a land sacred to both the Greek and the Roman Churches.

The Pope was indeed interested. He wanted to keep the Moslems as far as possible from European shores. There was a possibility, too, that a victory over the Seljuks, brought about by the aid of the Pope, might even bring the Greek Catholics into the Roman Church. A religious war could also be of help to the Pope in the struggle he was having with the kings of Europe, who were beginning to object that the Church was interfering in the civil affairs of their realms. If thousands of faithful Catholics could be brought together, armed and inspired to fight for the greater glory of the Church, no king would dare to question the authority of the Pope, even in purely economic and political affairs.

So Pope Urban began to preach the first Crusade in 1095, calling upon the Christians of Europe to fight the Moslems, promising forgiveness of sins for all who participated. His appeal aroused tremendous excitement. From all sides, from every village, hamlet and town, came thousands eager to defend the Faith. Wherever priests and monks preached the great Crusade, men left their homes and their families to enlist in the Holy War.

However, not all who joined the Crusade were inspired by religion. For some it was an opportunity to escape serfdom and its monotonous life. For some it meant a chance to go on a long journey full of adventure. Others hoped to become powerful lords by conquering land from the Moslems and establishing themselves as rulers there. There were also many criminals in the crusading army, since even lawbreakers had been urged to become "soldiers of Christ."

The army of 300,000 that responded to the call for the

Crusade thus had a peculiar mingling of devout Catholics and irresponsible hangers-on. On their march through Europe toward the ports of embarkation, the zeal of the Crusaders was brought to fever pitch by fiery speeches and sermons against the enemies of the Church. The Crusaders did not wait until they reached Mohammedan territory to express their zeal; when their route brought them near quiet and modest Jewish settlements in France, Germany, and Italy, mobs of Crusaders rampaged and slaughtered their way through the communities. Now, at last, the centuries of planting hatred against Jews and Judaism bore its bloody fruit. The animus against Jews, which had been the theme song of countless teachers, preachers, and orators ever since the days of Saint Paul, produced its harvest. For by the time of the Crusade practically all of Europe was Christian, and many who had never had contact with Jews nevertheless carried suspicion and hatred of Jews in their hearts.

For four long, anguished months, the Jewish communities felt the sword and the torch, both wielded in the name of Jesus! Even when the Jews tried to escape the fury of the mobs by seeking refuge in the palace of the bishop, as they did in the town of Worms, in Germany, for instance, it did not help. The Bishop of Worms pleaded with the Crusaders to have mercy, in the name of Christianity, and to save their passion for the Moslems. Words were unavailing; the mob broke into the bishop's palace, slaughtered the Jews on the spot, except those who consented to be baptized into Christianity. Scenes such as this were repeated in many towns. A few appeals for mercy, even by bishops, could not undo the hatred that had been bred throughout the centuries.

Under the Cross

By the time the frenzy was over, and the Crusaders were again on the march to the East to fight the Seljuks, most of the Jewish communities lay in ruins. Here and there in Europe, Christian rulers permitted Jews who had been baptized at the point of a sword to revert to Judaism. But in most places, no "back sliding" was allowed. Here and there, also, some of the property that had been stolen from the Jews was returned. In most places, however, the Jews had to start from scratch to reorganize their shattered lives.

Gradually the survivors forgot the scars and the terror; and just as life approached normalcy, a second Crusade was launched, in the year 1147. Again the sermons and agitation, again the zeal, again the outpouring of the faithful; and again the bloody attacks upon the Jews in the path of the Crusaders. There were a number of other Crusades in the next hundred years or so, and each spelled disaster for the Jews; each was a nightmare of horror.

Besides religious fanaticism, economic envy lay at the root of the hatred that was made to sprout in the hearts of the Crusaders and their leaders. The Jews had been forced into moneylending and trade, while the others made their living as farmers. The agricultural communities of Europe were self-sufficient, even though the serfs were by no means prosperous. Money was not an important commodity since the manorial estates produced whatever the people of the villages required for their use. At the fairs and markets they bartered surplus goods for articles they could not make.

The need for equipping the army of Crusaders put money and supplies at a premium. Merchandizing and moneylending became quite profitable. Since Jews had established themselves in both these businesses, Christian merchants benefited when a thriving Jewish community was ruined; it neatly eliminated Jewish competition. Envious Christian merchants found it useful, therefore, to stir up the unfavorable emotional attitude toward Jews that the Church had fostered.

Lords and others who were in debt to Jews also found the hostile attitude toward Jews useful to them. They saw to it that the Crusader mobs who stormed the palaces and cathedrals of the bishops would do more than merely slaughter and baptize the Jews within; they saw to it that all the records of their indebtedness to the Jews, which were kept in the cathedrals for safekeeping, were burned. No records—no need to repay the debt. And if the Jewish moneylender perished in the attack, the lord would be even more pleased.

One of the things the Church did during the Crusades helped considerably to channelize the religious fervor of Europe into hateful streams against the Jews. The Popes, to get volunteers, canceled all interest payments for any Crusader who was in debt to a Jew. King Louis IX of France, who supported the Church and the Crusades, went further than that: he absolved Crusaders of their debts to Jews altogether. Such offhand treatment of Jews as people possessing no rights that Christians needed to respect, as people who need not be treated the way other human beings were, blunted the moral sense of the Crusaders; it permitted them to hack at Jews without a twinge to their consciences.

Europe, however, did gain something from the Crusades:

trade between East and West began to flourish and European cities grew rapidly. New goods, new skills, new ideas from Mohammedan lands enriched the European continent. Such Arabic words as algebra, coffee, syrup, almanac, sofa, sherbet, and the very Arabic numbers we use today, attest to the influence of the East upon Western civilization. But these gains came as a result of hitherto unparalleled bloodshed. Europe was enriched both materially and culturally, but the East was impoverished in these respects. Arab and Mohammedan civilization began to decline rapidly as a result of the numerous wars the Church fought on the soil of the Moslems. Their lands and resources were taken from them, their centers of learning were destroyed, the people were left poor and the countries disorganized.

An increasing number of Christians began to engage in large-scale trade and moneylending, which took on the nature of modern banking. Loans were not made for personal needs, but rather for business, to encourage large-scale commerce. But the Church had decreed that the charging of interest for loans to fellow Christians was contrary to Christian doctrine and belief. It had permitted Jews to charge interest only because they were, in the words of St. Thomas Aquinas, "so helplessly damned that no crime could aggravate their condition." But when the growth of trade made banking a vital business in Europe, the Church changed its attitude in the matter of the charging of interest. The former Jewish monopoly came to an end, and the bulk of the banking business passed into the hands of Christians, particularly the Lombards.

Christians also began to dominate the trade of Europe, especially in the West. In some areas Jews had been tolerated, even sought after, because they fulfilled a necessary function as traders. But when Christians began to do this work, the Jews were no longer needed. Lords and kings, therefore, no longer were eager to protect their Jews, whose industry had previously enriched them. Others could replace them now—Christians. In fact, the Christians who wanted to replace them clamored for the expulsion of the Jews altogether. And there was a wave of expulsions in the thirteenth, fourteenth, and fifteenth centuries. In France, in England, in the various states and cities of Germany, the Jews were ordered to pack up and leave.

Old, established Jewish communities were thus uprooted, and the days of Jewish homelessness and wandering began. Not only were the Jews affected physically; their spiritual outlook, their culture, their way of life were also affected. This new chapter in Jewish history is of key importance in its influence upon the molding of the modern Jew.

CHAPTER ELEVEN

The Ghetto Years

*T*HE dominant force in Europe during the Middle Ages was the Church. From its teaching came the idea that man entered the world a sinner; his soul was forfeit unless he was "saved" by the Church, whose rituals and sacraments were the only keys to the Kingdom of Heaven. Church leaders therefore regarded it as their mission to bring all people into the fold. Pope Gregory I (590–604) and other Church leaders urged missionaries to win converts through persuasive and convincing argument, but thousands of Jews were forced to undergo baptism during the Crusades on pain of death.

The Jews were not the only ones with religious beliefs and practices that differed from those of the Church. There were Christians who did not see eye to eye with the Roman Catholic Church's interpretation of Christianity. Some refused to accept the Pope's decision as final in all matters concerning the faith. There were some Christians who disagreed with certain theological doctrines of the Church, or questioned various practices that had been decreed by the Church authorities over the years. These dissidents the Church regarded as "heretics." All such Christians were persecuted by the Popes and bishops, who saw in heresy a threat to the authority of the Church.

The Roman Church was more than a spiritual power in the Middle Ages; it was a worldly power as well, owning large estates in many parts of Europe. Its officials were rulers just like other lords. In Church lands they had political as well as religious authority; the people they ruled owed them the same feudal services and military aid that serfs on private estates owed to their lords. The Church's decrees were, therefore, frequently both religious and political. People who objected to the political activities of Church officials were just as much heretics in the eyes of the Church as those who objected to religious doctrines or practices. For in that undemocratic period, the emphasis was upon conformity, and Church officials, no less than lords and kings, tried to suppress all doubters and questioners.

The Church's opposition to heresy was so great that many violent attacks were made upon nonconforming Christian groups. A particularly bloody attack took place in 1208, in southern France, where a large number of Christians called the Albigenses lived. They questioned various Church doctrines, including those relating to the Holy Ghost. The campaign of Pope Innocent III against the Albigensian heresy took on the nature of a "crusade" which resulted in the slaughtering of large numbers of them. But in spite of this and other attacks, many Christians in Europe still persisted in their nonconformist religious activities. In the 1230's, therefore, Pope Gregory IX decided to establish a special body, the Inquisition, to devote itself to the one task of ferreting out and punishing heretics.

With the Church engaged in such an all-out struggle against Christians who did not accept every item in the Catholic way of worship, the Jews could not remain unscathed, since they were the archnonconformists of the time, being completely outside the Christian fold. No direct crusades were preached against them, but Jews who refused to accept Christianity faced the alternative of death, as in the period of the Crusades; or continual persecution; or expulsion from the states they lived in. Under such pressure, many Jews in France, England, Spain, and elsewhere underwent baptism. But even larger numbers committed suicide rather than give up Judaism. In Worms, Speyer, Esslingen, Vienna, Frankfurt, York, and in countless other European towns, whole communities of Jews locked themselves in their synagogues and set them on fire, when mobs attacked, praying to the very end in their own way, rather than accept Christianity. During this period of the thirteenth and fourteenth centuries, the Jewish population of Europe was decimated.

The pressure against Jews and heretics became particularly strong when Christians were entering trade and commerce in larger numbers. Before the Church made it legal for Christians to charge interest for loans, many towns had urged Jews to settle in their localities to build up the trade of those places. Now, however, with Christians eager to handle the moneylending and trade, the welcome mat for Jews was removed from the gates of many cities. In fact, Christian merchants and moneylenders urged the authorities to expel the Jews altogether, so they could take over their business. For the same reasons they also favored attacks upon heretics, since many of them also happened to be merchants.

The Church's drive against heretics and Jews was thus a handy weapon by which Christian merchants could eliminate competition and enrich themselves. It was also handy for nobles and kings, since the property left by those who were liquidated or expelled accrued to them. Ferdinand and Isabella, who ruled two of the greatest provinces of Spain, reaped especially great profit from the campaign against heresy.

For a long time, it had been the custom for the nobles of Spain to select their king. Since they could withdraw their support whenever they disagreed with the chosen ruler, the king of Spain was never really the unquestioned authority in the country. Ferdinand, who wanted to bring the entire land under his rule, introduced the Inquisition into Spain in 1480, and used it as a club to stifle all opposition against him.

Through the Inquisition, Ferdinand got what he wanted. He had only to accuse his enemies and they would be hailed before the Court of the Inquisition, where they would have to prove their loyalty to the Church, a rather difficult task since the Inquisitors acted as judge, jury, and prosecuting attorney. A reign of terror descended upon the land; few dared to speak their minds, to criticize either the Church or the king. Those who did were burned at the stake. A businessman need only whisper that his Christian competitor was a heretic—he did not have to give evidence to show there was a basis for the accusation—and the Inquisition did the rest. Very few ever succeeded in proving themselves innocent.

When a victim of the Inquisition was burned at the stake, his property was confiscated and turned over to the royal treasury. The records show that even people who were dead and buried were brought to trial for having been heretics during their lifetimes. If pronounced guilty, the bodies were exhumed and then publicly and ceremoniously burned; the property they once had owned then reverted to the king!

When Torquemada, Isabella's personal religious guide, became the head of the Inquisition, the terror was intensified. Torquemada investigated not only a person's religious practices, but also his thoughts and beliefs. Under such scrutiny nobody was safe. It took only twelve years of the Inquisition to make Ferdinand and Isabella the undisputed rulers of Spain.

Although all Christians in Spain had become Roman Catholic in practice, Torquemada and Isabella were not satisfied. They wanted to make Spain completely Catholic. So they prevailed upon Ferdinand to expel the Jews and Moors. The Jews were ordered out of the country on March 31, 1492, and were given four months to arrange their affairs. They were forbidden to take gold, silver, or precious stones out of the country; they naturally had to leave behind houses, fields, and other immovable property, all of which became the property of the king.

Their synagogues were converted into churches; the stones of their cemeteries were used in the erection of public buildings; and their community houses were converted to whatever use the king decided. The same fate met the products of Mohammedan life and culture after the Moors were expelled.

Thus came to an end the Jewish community in Spain. For centuries, the Jews had been an important part of Spain's life, a people who had contributed a great deal to the material and cultural upbuilding of the country. In the year Columbus discovered America—in fact the four months of grace the king gave the Jews ended the day before he sailed—the Spanish Jews were driven from their homeland.

Finding a place in which to live was now indeed a problem for the Jews. Some cities and states of Europe simply refused them permission to enter. A number of Jews became pioneers in Brazil, the West Indies, and other parts of the newly-discovered continent of South America, and some went to North Africa and other Mohammedan regions. Holland and other countries of Europe, where the rulers wanted their trade and commerce developed, did accept Jews, for they had the "know-how" of trade from long experience. The townspeople of Antwerp, Belgium, for instance, petitioned their king to admit Jews, declaring "that by the trade they will expand far beyond the present limits, the benefits derived will be for the good of the whole land, and gold and silver will be available in greater quantities for the needs of the state."

But it was not their love for the Jews—nor even a humanitarian feeling for the "underdog"—that prompted these Christians to permit Jews to come in. It was plain, hardheaded business considerations. The kings of Poland, for just such reasons, issued special invitations to Jews to settle in that country, and a great many Jews came to

Poland, particularly in the sixteenth and seventeenth centuries.

But this kind of hospitality was not generally extended in western Europe where the Christian merchant class wanted no competition from the Jews. In that part of Europe, particularly in Germany, Austria, and Italy, the Jews were segregated from the Christian population; they were forced to live in walled-off communities called "ghettos." The Church had ordered the establishment of such ghettos to keep Christians from being "tainted" by close association with Jews.

The merchant class was quite satisfied to see that the decree was enforced, and by the end of the sixteenth century the vast majority of Europe's Jews had been forced into ghettos.

The ghettos were set up in the least desirable parts of the towns; in swampy sections and in dark and narrow streets. The space allotted the Jews was always too small for the number who were forced to live in it. And if it was not unhealthy right from the start, it soon became an unsanitary slum, since it could not be enlarged even though the population increased. Every inch of space had to be used for buildings, and the houses themselves had to be built higher and higher until there was little light or air for the people who lived in them.

The ghettos were generally separated from the rest of the town by walls, with gates that were locked on the outside, which the city authorities usually kept closed at night, on Sundays, and on Christian holidays. And sad was the lot of the Jew who returned to the ghetto after the gates had been locked!

Special decrees defined the rights and duties of Jews. Mostly, the laws contained restrictions, some harsh, some more lenient. In some places, they were graciously permitted to sit and rest awhile when they entered the city for business purposes, although they were under orders not to spend more time in the town than was necessary. In some towns they were restricted to walking in the gutters. Everywhere they were forced to wear "Jew badges" when they stepped out of the ghetto. There was a limit set to the number of families that could reside within the gates of certain towns; limitations were even placed on the number of Jews who were permitted to marry during the year! At least once a year, in a number of ghettos, the Jews were required to assemble in their synagogues to listen to a conversion sermon delivered by a Catholic priest.

And then there were taxes—a multitude of them. If a Jew had to enter a town on business he paid a tax; and another when he left the town. Here he was taxed to cross a bridge and there to cross a frontier. There were special taxes for Jews twelve years or older, and additional special taxes whenever the lord or king was short of cash.

It was easy to tax the Jew for he had virtually no rights. Even his right to live in the ghetto depended upon his obtaining a license—for a fee. The license was usually issued for a limited period and had to be renewed from time to time; each renewal meant the payment of another fee.

And yet, as restricted as was his life, despite his lack of freedom, he was still better off in the ghettos than he had been during the nightmare of the Crusades. Hemmed in though he was in the ghetto, it was nevertheless better than being a homeless wanderer. Within the ghettos, moreover, the Jews were permitted to carry on a variety of business enterprises. In some, as in the ghetto of Venice, Italy, Jews employed hundreds of Christians within their gates. And during the day, when the gates were open, there were streams of Gentiles who came in to shop and trade.

The ghetto offered certain advantages to the Jews. Within its walls they enjoyed a certain degree of security. But what was far more important, it welded the Jews into a compact group and made it possible for them to organize their life according to the rules of the Talmud, for each ghetto was given the right to govern itself. Beyond the walls might lie a hostile world; inside the gate the Jew could live a Jewish life. When its gates closed upon him, he felt that he was at home, among his own, and there was restored to him a feeling that he belonged. In the security of his ghetto, whose gates shut off the hostile world, he regained a sense of his own dignity and worth. In the ghetto he was an accepted member of society.

The ghettos were ruled by Jewish councils whose members were usually elected by the property owners of the community. The councils were in charge of maintaining law and order, but they also governed practically every activity the people engaged in. Even though it was a law dealing with religious practices, such as the prohibition of the singing of popular songs on important fast days; or one dealing with business matters, like the setting up of a limit to the amount of commission a broker could charge; even if the law dealt with purely social activities, such as the kind of clothing a Jewish woman should wear, the council's regulations were accepted without question by the Jews as the rule for Jewish living.

The most important members of the councils were the religious leaders, who made their decisions and regulations on the basis of the laws of the Talmud. Just as lawyers today cite previous decisions of judges to show that their arguments are sound, so did the community councils cite the decisions of the Rabbis of the Talmud to show that their laws were in keeping with the spirit of the religion. The people accepted the regulations since they regarded the Talmud and its interpretations as the word of God, as statutes and ordinances to guide every phase of their lives.

There were some Jews, however, who broke the laws of the councils; the Jewish courts of the ghetto took care of them, meting out fines or sentencing them to corporal punishment. A serious breach might even result in the excommunication of the offender. He would be ordered to dress in mourning clothes and appear before a gathering in the synagogue, where the reasons for the excommunication would be publicly announced, the candlelights would be extinguished, and the *shofar*, the ram's horn that is used only on the High Holy Days, would be blown. After that he was treated like an outcast, not being permitted to associate with the people of the community. In a time when Jews were not free to move from one neighborhood to another, this was indeed a cruel punishment.

The Christian authorities restricted Jewish life outside the ghettos, and the Jewish authorities restricted it inside. One might get the impression that, between the two, ghetto life was rather dreary, weighted down by a multitude of rules and obligations. But this was not true, for most of the councils tried to make life comfortable and pleasant for the people, often providing special community kitchens where a family could prepare for a happy celebration or a wedding feast, affairs that the average ghetto apartment could not accommodate. Some communities built special bathhouses, not only for personal cleanliness but also for ritual purposes (to prepare oneself for the Sabbath and Holy days). They also provided community wells for water. In many a ghetto there was even a dance hall, for dancing was a popular pastime among the Jews.

Compared to the towns and villages around them, the ghettos were actually lively places to live in. There was a continual interchange of ideas as Jewish merchants traveled from ghetto to ghetto, bringing with them news and views from other parts of the world. But more than anything else, the festivals of the Jews brought a lively excitement into their communal life. There was a carnival spirit at Purim time, the holiday that commemorates the saving of the Persian Jews from extermination at the hands of Haman, the Persian prime minister in the days of King Ahasuerus and Queen Esther. Even the rabbi could be mimicked or caricatured without fear at Purim time, a festival the Jews celebrated gaily. There was Hanukkah, also full of fun, especially for the children, and Passover, with its festive Seder, a time for a grand family reunion. Jewish life was not restricted to services at the synagogue; its many festivals and ceremonies were likewise observed in the home.

There was a spirit of helpfulness in the ghettos too. In each ghetto a *Chevrah Kedushah* (Holy League) was organized, the members of which visited those who were ill to see that their needs were looked after and to cheer them up. And because so many families had been uprooted and impoverished by expulsions and restrictions, the community councils made it almost their main business to see that the needy were provided for. The funds for these charities were collected from all the Jews as a regular tax. The giving of alms was considered by rich and poor alike to be a religious duty.

The Jew of the seventeenth century had no freedom or rights; neither did he have duties or responsibilities in the affairs of the outside world. His main concern was to live within his own community according to his religion. The ghetto became his world; within its walls he lived a completely Jewish life, every phase of it governed by the traditional laws of his people.

With nothing to gain from contact with Christian society except humiliation, he quite naturally became indifferent to the Gentile world. Forced to live apart from the Christians, he began, as they did, to look upon himself as someone apart, different from the rest of the people of Europe. Since the Jew was not permitted to share their joys and sorrows and hopes, his feelings and interests became centered in his own community. He was a Jew, and all the others were Gentiles—*Goyim*. The ghetto became a wall that barred him from European life. As a result, ghetto Jews had but little contact with the ideas that were becoming current in the Christian world.

The Jews of the Mohammedan world had mingled freely with their neighbors as self-respecting citizens, interested in all that went on about them. In such an atmosphere, Judah Halevi of Spain had been able to write brilliant poetry, as well as philosophical studies about the meaning of religion and life. He discussed Judaism, Christianity, and

Mohammedanism in his great work *The Cuzari* which he
wrote in Arabic in 1140, pointing out the contributions
the three faiths were making toward building the world of
brotherhood and mutual helpfulness the Prophets had
talked about.

In Egypt, also a part of the Mohammedan world, lived
another Jew, the great Moses Maimonides, whose interests
were also not limited to strictly Jewish affairs. In his time,
toward the end of the twelfth century, Mohammedan and
Jewish religious leaders were troubled by the teachings of
philosophers which seemed to contradict the Bible. The
world, said the philosophers, was "eternal"—it had always
existed. But the Bible said that God created the world out
of nothing. Maimonides, in one of his many profound
books, showed that there was no contradiction in the two
ideas. Both the world and God were eternal, he pointed
out; what God did was to give the world form and purpose.

This book, *The Guide to the Perplexed*, was written in
Arabic, and was studied by Jews and Mohammedans. It was
translated into Latin and other languages, enabling many
Christian scholars and churchmen to read it. Maimonides
was thus able to make a contribution to Christian thought,
since Christian theologians in Europe also had to settle
the seeming conflict between Faith and Reason (today we
would call it the conflict between Religion and Science).
Thomas Aquinas, the great Catholic theologian adopted
the ideas of Maimonides, even acknowledging his indebtedness to him.

The Christian world was indebted to other Jews as well
for some of its concepts and ideas. In fact, for centuries

Christian theologians and scholars studied as part of Catholic philosophy a book that was actually written by a Jew. The book was *Fons Vitae* (The Fountain of Life), written by Solomon ibn Gabirol of Spain about the year 1050. When the book was translated from Arabic into Latin, the author's name for some reason was given as Avicebron. It contained such beautiful thoughts and ideas that Christian scholars believed it had been written by a Catholic philosopher. Not until the nineteenth century was it discovered that ibn Gabirol was the real author.

Through the works of ibn Gabirol, Judah Halevi, Maimonides, and many others, Jews had been able to make important contributions to the knowledge and thought of the world. These men were able to do so because they were part of the world; they were not confined to a little corner of it. They lived with their neighbors, and like them were interested in everything that went on. But the ghetto was not a good soil for the cultivation of noble philosophy or thoughts about the meaning of life. The ghetto Jews had enough to occupy their minds just trying to solve the problems of everyday living, made so difficult for them by a hostile world. For centuries they had been a people who had enriched the culture of the world; now they were becoming narrow in outlook, limited in their horizon to the life within the ghetto walls. The ghetto became their world, and only what went on within it seemed to matter to them.

It was only natural, then, that the schools of the ghetto should pay less and less attention to higher mathematics and philosophy, even to the languages of European culture. The Jews, once familiar with Greek, Arabic, and

The Ghetto Years

Latin, now required only Yiddish, the language used for everyday intercourse, and Hebrew for prayers and services and the study of the Bible and the Talmud.

In centuries past the Jews had continually elaborated the Talmud, bringing it up to date in the light of the knowledge around them. But from 1567 on, when Joseph Caro wrote the SHULCHAN ARUCH, a codification of Talmudic law, the further development of the Talmud stopped. The hundreds of laws Caro listed, laws that regulated almost every act of a Jew's life, were accepted as the final word and authority in Judaism. The Shulchan Aruch became the "Bible" that ghetto students spent their lives mastering. For most Jews, Judaism had come to mean little more than obeying of rules of ceremonial and ritual observance as laid down in the Shulchan Aruch, and it was considered irreligious or impious to violate them in any way.

Like the leaders of the Church, who tried to restrain all who questioned its doctrines and practices, the rabbis and leaders of the ghettos punished Jews who disagreed with the tradition as expressed in the Shulchan Aruch. Even in Amsterdam, Holland, where the Jews enjoyed more freedom than in other European areas, Uriel Acosta was excommunicated in 1616 for challenging some of the beliefs held by Jews.

Acosta was descended from a Jewish family that had fled the Inquisition. While in Portugal they had been forced to become converted to Christianity. But they became Marranos—outwardly they lived as Christians, but secretly they observed as many Jewish religious ceremonials as they could. By the time Uriel was born, the Acosta family had become almost completely Christian, and he was sent to a college to prepare for the priesthood. He disagreed with some of the teachings of Christianity, and when he learned of his Jewish past he convinced his family to return to the faith of his ancestors. To live openly as Jews they had to flee, and went to Holland where they could live in peace.

But Uriel Acosta objected also to the strict rules of the Talmud, and challenged the beliefs held by many Jews of that day about immortality, resurrection, and other matters dealing with life after death. For seven years after his excommunication, Acosta was shunned by his neighbors. To be re-admitted to the good graces of the community, he made a public confession of guilt, but he was broken by the shame and humiliation of it all, and after writing his autobiography committed suicide.

The same Amsterdam community excommunicated the youthful Baruch Spinoza, who later became a famous philosopher, in 1656. The leaders were not so concerned that his ideas conflicted with Jewish teaching; in Spinoza's case, it was the fear that his philosophic ideas might offend Christians, and would cause attacks upon the Jewish community as a whole.

It had not been a tradition in Jewish life to force all Jews to think alike. There were no fixed dogmas; the Jews had always enjoyed intellectual freedom, for there had always been room for interpretation and change. But the ghettos forced the Jews to develop a pattern of life based on "dogmas" and rigid observance, a special pattern of their own since they were forced to live separate and apart from the Christian world.

Outside the ghettos, meanwhile, from the sixteenth century on, Europe was beginning to shake the sleep of the

Middle Ages out of its eyes, as a result of the Renaissance and the Protestant Reformation. But the Jews practically stood still, intellectually. A strange situation indeed! For the very ideas that were beginning to make Europeans more reasonable and intelligent had come to Europe in some measure through the Jews themselves.

Throughout the Middle Ages, Europeans had been almost exclusively concerned with the study of Christian theology. So far as Christian Europe was concerned, the science of mathematics, the philosophic, historical, and scientific works of the great ancient writers had become extinct. But the Arabs had translated these ancient works into Arabic and had been studying them all through the early Middle Ages.

When Europeans came in close contact with the East, through the Crusades and through trade, they began to learn of this great body of knowledge. But it was in a language the scholars of Europe did not know too well. Jewish scholars, who knew both Arabic and the classical languages, were called upon to translate these books. Their work made the treasures of ancient Greek poetry, philosophy, and other literature available to the Christian world. Jewish scholars thus helped pull Europe out of the "Dark Ages."

Besides their contributions to European culture as translators, the Jews had also helped in the awakening of Europe by their very history as recorded in the Bible. When the Jewish Bible was translated into the different European tongues, along with the New Testament, people were able to read and study the Old Testament for themselves, instead of depending upon the excerpts read to them from the Latin version by the priests. They became more aware of the social ideas of the Prophets, of their championing of the common man in the name of God. This aspect of the Prophets had been neglected to a large extent by Christian theologians in the early Middle Ages, for they had concentrated their attention on selected passages from the books of the Prophets, on those words and phrases they interpreted as foretelling the coming of Jesus. But the birth of the Protestant faith in the sixteenth century gave a new emphasis to the meaning of the Prophets, a new importance to the Old Testament altogether. The Hebrew Bible was actually part of the intellectual ferment in Europe.

The ferment in the ghettos, however, born of the humiliation and economic suffering that had been forced upon the Jews, was expressed in the yearning for the Messiah, who had become to the average Jew a sort of miracle man, who would lift them out of their degradation.

Some Jews imagined that the expected leader was slow in coming because he was in some way bewitched—like the heroes and heroines of fairy tales who are held in a magical spell that cannot be broken until someone does the things that are required to free them. Most people in the medieval period were full of superstitious beliefs in miracles and spirits. Some Jews, believing that the Messiah could not come unless he were freed of the bonds that held him, pored over sacred Jewish writings looking for words or phrases that might be the magic passwords. They looked for combinations of letters that might add up to some magical formula. Speculations such as these engaged the rapt attention of many educated Jews at the very time European scholars were devoting their energies to the study of science and philosophy.

Knowing how anxiously Jews yearned for the God-given leader, many an impostor arose to claim that he was the promised Messiah. The most famous of these false Messiahs was Shabbatai Zevi, who was born in the Turkish city of Smyrna. He came to believe, because of his mathematical formulas, that the year of deliverance would occur in 1666.

When a brutal massacre of Jews occurred in the Ukraine in 1648, Shabbatai called it a sign of the coming of the Messiah. He then publicly pronounced the Hebrew name of God (Jahweh), something only the high priest of the Temple at Jerusalem in Hebrew times was permitted to do, and then only on Yom Kippur, the Day of Atonement. But Shabbatai, claiming to be the Messiah, announced that the ancient prohibition against the pronouncing of God's name was abolished.

The Jews shunned him for this act, and he was excommunicated. He made his way to Palestine, where he and his ideas met a friendlier reception. Some of his followers wrote many pamphlets about him and sent them to Jewish communities all over the world. By the year 1665, when Shabbatai returned to his native city of Smyrna, the very community that had banned him, the Jews there wildly acclaimed him. On Rosh Hashanah of that year, he was hailed as King and Messiah, in a celebration in which Jewish representatives from a number of other countries took part.

This occurred at a time of great trouble in the Jewish world. Austrian Jews were being persecuted by the Jesuits; Jews were being threatened with expulsion in various lands; and Jewish community life in Poland had been weakened by bloody attacks. The thought of a Messianic deliverance was a powerful stimulant to the Jews of the hard-pressed ghettos of Europe.

As the year 1666 approached, the Jews grew more and more excited. The Turkish government, fearful that the Jews in its domain might stage a revolt under the leadership of Shabbatai, arrested him. To many of his followers, this was proof that he was the Messiah, that Shabbatai was being made to suffer for their sins. Even when it was learned that Shabbatai had turned Mohammedan in order to escape execution, many Jews could not bring themselves to give up hope. But the fever subsided with the years, and the movement Shabbatai had inspired fell apart.

During the seventeenth century, as the European mind was gradually becoming unfettered and accepting new truths, the Jewish mind was becoming more and more fettered. Ghetto life was hemmed in by the inflexible legal rules laid down in the Talmud and by the multitude of restrictions the Christian rulers had ringed round the Jews. Ghetto dwellers fell prey to superstitious beliefs, to futile hopes for miracles. While European scholars were laying the groundwork for the great scientific revolution, Jewish scholars were engaged in mystical studies in search of magical formulas for the coming of the Messiah, and in fantastic speculations on the joys of the future life. The world lost something too, not just the Jews. For a Maimonides, or a Gabirol, could not easily develop in the limited horizon of the ghetto.

The ghetto had been devised as a physical barrier to separate the Jews from their Christian neighbors; it became with the years, a mental wall around the Jewish mind, separating Jewish thought from the world of ideas outside the gates.

CHAPTER TWELVE

The Emancipation of the Jews

GREAT social and economic changes were taking place in Europe during the ghetto centuries. The rise of world-wide trade shifted the center of European life from the isolated, self-sufficient agricultural estates to the thriving towns and cities. Craftsmen and artisans began to grow in importance, to assume a more significant place in the scheme of society. A new class of wealthy merchants and manufacturers developed, men who resented the privileges of the feudal lords, privileges that were reserved for the nobility and clergy alone. The business leaders began to demand the rights enjoyed by the favored classes.

All through the feudal period kings had fought many wars against independent, powerful lords in their lands, to bring them under direct control of the crown. Gradually, people dropped the allegiance they had owed the lords of the estates they lived on; they began to think of themselves as subjects of the king who represented the nation, rather than as "men" of a particular lord, tied to the territory he ruled.

The kings, however, did not claim the sole loyalty of their subjects, for the people also owed allegiance to the Pope. Many kings resented this, for the Pope, besides being the religious head of the Church, was also a king. He was the ruler over vast estates, concerned as much with the material wealth and property of the Church as with the spiritual welfare of its communicants. Within Church lands, he had the power to tax and make laws like any king. But he also collected taxes for the Church in lands over which the Church did not rule, and large amounts of money flowed from them annually to Rome.

Most of the kings had no quarrel with the religious doctrines of the Church; they accepted the Pope's authority in that field. They did object to the civil and political powers that the Pope exerted within their countries through his bishops and archbishops. Besides wanting to have complete power over their subjects, the kings would have liked to keep under control the money that went to Rome from their own lands. And many a king cast a longing eye upon the property of the Church within his state, property he could not tax but would have loved to.

While kings were troubled by the economic and political power of the Church, other Christians were becoming increasingly concerned about the doctrines of the Church. Along with the goods that were entering Europe from the East had come new books and ideas. Some of the new learning contradicted the traditional teachings of the Church, which led many scholars to question the accepted truths of their time. The leaders of the Church attacked them for doubting official Church doctrines; some of the scholars then denied the right of the Church to stop them from questioning, which they regarded as an important step toward real truth.

It took courage in those days to do this. For to question what the Church held to be true, or to criticize the practices of the Church or its officials, often brought severe penalties upon those who did so. Nevertheless, John Wycliffe, an English priest of the fourteenth century, insisted that some Christian practices were based on superstition, not true religion. He questioned the truth of certain Church doctrines, and even denied that the Pope could exercise any authority except as he acted according to the Gospels. To him, the Bible was the only true authority.

Since few Englishmen could read the Latin version of the Bible, Wycliffe translated it into English, so that more of his countrymen could read it for themselves, and judge between the Church and himself. John Huss, a Bohemian, and other scholars were influenced by Wycliffe's teaching. The Bible was translated into other languages, and after the printing press was invented in the middle of the fifteenth century, larger numbers of Bibles became available for home reading.

By the beginning of the sixteenth century, many Europeans were no longer ready, as their medieval ancestors had been, to accept ideas merely because the Church said they were true. Some even questioned the Church's attitude toward the Jews! In the year 1509, for instance, Maximilian, Emperior of Austria, was asked by the Christian clergy to burn the Talmud, because they claimed it was full of hostile lies about Christianity. But their word was no longer enough. Maximilian called in Johann Reuchlin, a respected Christian scholar, to check up on the facts. Reuchlin, who knew Hebrew well, gave the Talmud a clean bill of health and even suggested that the emperor provide each university with two professors of Hebrew; to him a knowledge of that language was necessary for a proper understanding of Christianity, since so much of it was based on the history and ideas of the Jews.

Maximilian's refusal to burn the Talmud, and Reuchlin's espousal of Hebrew, irked some of the representatives of the Church. They launched a campaign of attack against Reuchlin and his ideas. Many Christian scholars came to Reuchlin's defense, and a religious controversy ensued. During the debate many doctrines and practices of the Church were critically analyzed, and many passages of the Bible were given unorthodox interpretations. Thus, the attention of people was drawn more and more to the Bible as an important source of religious ideas. Many of the common people, not only the scholars, began to question the traditional interpretations the Church had made of it, particularly of the Old Testament.

At this time, too, people began more openly to criticize the behavior of high officials of the Church, some of whom were devoting themselves to the pleasures of the flesh rather than to the spiritual needs of the people. From kings who resented the economic and political power of the Church; from scholarly priests who believed that the Church was in error in many of its beliefs and practices; and from people in various other walks of life came a certain amount of antagonism and opposition to the Church. And in the year 1517 all the resentment, whatever its source, came to a head.

The Emancipation of the Jews

In that year a Catholic monk by the name of Martin Luther openly condemned the practice of granting indulgences (freedom from suffering in purgatory for sins committed during one's lifetime) to those who made money contributions toward the Pope's project of rebuilding St. Peter's Cathedral in Rome. Luther called the indulgences licenses to commit sin, since all a person had to do to escape punishment for sins was to make a donation.

Luther's protest led to heated debate all over Europe, and the accumulated doubts that had been suppressed by people's fear that the Church might withhold salvation from them, now spilled over the dam. People began to state openly, as Luther had done, that the Pope's decrees were not religious laws that had to be obeyed in the interest of winning salvation. They argued that only the Bible was the word of God, and every individual, not the Pope alone, could interpret the word of God.

Now, Luther was a Catholic monk who loved his religion; he hoped that his criticisms would lead to the correction of what he felt were incorrect religious ideas and practices. But the Pope, hoping to put an end to the rising tide of criticism of the religion, ordered Luther to recant— to admit publicly that he had erred in attacking the practices of the Church—on pain of excommunication as a heretic. Luther refused, saying that he would not change his opinions unless it could be shown in the Bible itself that he was wrong. He translated the Bible into German so that the people of his country could read it and see that his conception of Christianity was truly in accordance with Scripture.

As a result of this conflict, Europe's Christians came to

be divided into two camps, into two separate and distinct Christian faiths. One group remained faithful to the Pope and the traditional doctrines of the Roman Church, while the Protestants (as those who protested against these doctrines were called) denied the authority of the Pope over them.

Then, for a century and a half European life was disrupted by wars between Roman Catholics and Protestants. Countless books and pamphlets attacking either Catholic or Protestant beliefs appeared in every country. Gradually people grew tired of the never-ending religious controversies, for the endless disputes brought them confusion rather than a better understanding of life and the world. More and more they turned to the exciting, and more rewarding, knowledge that the scientists and philosophers were producing.

Scientists like Galileo and Sir Isaac Newton, by their observation and study of the operations of the universe, had reached conclusions that disproved many of the accepted ideas Europe had inherited from medieval times. Over many years various scientists had been proving that the universe operated according to natural laws; that nature was not controlled by secret and mysterious forces. They showed that knowledge gained through experimentation, rather than supernatural theories, could more satisfactorily explain what occurred in the natural world.

Philosophers, meanwhile, were examining the social conditions under which people lived, conditions Europeans had been taught for a long time to accept as normal and unchangeable. They rejected the traditional view of the Church that life on earth was merely a test, a proving ground for the next world. They questioned the accepted social and economic arrangement of society, which permitted the nobility to enjoy many privileges and luxuries while the great mass of Europeans slaved their lives away to eke out a miserable existence. They refused to accept the idea that kings and nobles ruled by Divine Right, and that it was therefore the duty of the common people to accept their lot because God willed it that way. Like the Hebrew Prophets who had denounced the unjust conditions of ancient times, the philosophers of the period of the Protestant Reformation attacked with indignation the evils they saw about them. Many of the stirring phrases of the Prophets were re-uttered in those days, as the campaign against autocracy and special privileges made headway.

John Locke, a Puritan philosopher in England, steeped in the study both of science and the Old Testament, proclaimed that all people, simply because they were human beings, possessed a natural right to life, liberty, and whatever property they acquired through their own labor. The whole purpose of government, he said, was to organize affairs in such a way that the people could enjoy these rights. And if the existing governments didn't give them their rights, then the people had the duty to change those governments and replace them with the kind of government that would look out for their interests!

These were pretty strong ideas for the 1670's and '80's. The common people of those days had practically no rights at all, no share in the government that ruled them. The fact that many people took Locke's ideas seriously, however, was a sign that Europe was awakening from its long medieval sleep.

Another great thinker, the Frenchman, Jean Jacques Rousseau, developed Locke's philosophy further. The Church had been teaching that man was by nature sinful and wicked, and that his only hope of escaping punishment for his original sinfulness was through the sacraments of the Church. Rousseau disagreed. He boldly stated (and it was a bold thing to do so in the early eighteenth century) that man came into the world equipped to do good. What caused man to turn to evil was not his original nature, which was neither evil nor good, but the environment he had to live in and the kind of education he received.

Rousseau attacked the social system of his time because it denied the common people their natural rights. He objected to the privileges of the clergy and nobility, and attacked the unequal distribution of wealth. He called it a bad society that permitted the enrichment of the few at the expense of the vast majority. He demanded a new approach to education; one that would make people more aware of their just rights and would make them strive to correct the evils of the social system.

Large numbers of people were stirred by the philosophers of the time. But the new viewpoint was not welcomed by the authorities. The aristocrats naturally did not want to share their wealth and privileges, and the Church felt that the new knowledge would cause people to have less faith in the doctrines it had been teaching for so many centuries. The antagonism against the new learning led to the persecution and hounding of many scholars and scientists.

Although many Europeans had already brushed the medieval cobwebs from their minds, a great many others regarded the new ideas with suspicion and fear. The air of

Europe was still full of intolerance toward new ideas, full of the prejudices that had been inherited from medieval times. In every generation, from early childhood people had been picking up unreasoning hates and suspicions, against Catholics, against Protestants, against Jews, against strangers, against anyone and anything different, and against any idea unconventional or new.

It was just this medieval spirit of intolerance and prejudice, that Voltaire, the great French thinker and writer, made war on. He kept hammering away at the need to study all points of view before coming to conclusions. He spent a fairly long life attacking intolerance, and even when he was sixty-eight years old, threw himself into a fight to right a wrong committed against the Calas family because of religious prejudice.

In the city of Toulouse, in France, in the year 1761, lived a shopkeeper by the name of Jean Calas, with his wife and four children. Calas was a Huguenot, a French Protestant, while most of his neighbors were Catholics.

One of his sons, Mark Anthony Calas, committed suicide by hanging himself in his father's shop. Shortly after his body was discovered, a rumor began to spread through the city that Mark Anthony had not committed suicide at all. The story that made the rounds was that Mark Anthony Calas had wanted to become a Catholic and that his father had killed him to prevent it. The whole city buzzed excitedly.

At the height of the hysteria, the city authorities brought Jean Calas to trial for the murder of his son. Not a shred of evidence was introduced to show that Jean Calas had had anything to do with his son's death. But the feeling in the city was so set against him and his fellow Huguenots, that he was declared guilty. He was executed by being broken on the wheel; his property was confiscated; his two daughters were ordered to a convent to be brought up as nuns; and his remaining son was sent to a monastery to become a monk.

A few months after the sentences had been carried out the case came to Voltaire's attention. Voltaire was a Catholic, but he felt it to be his duty to show the people of Toulouse how vicious and unjust they had become through intolerance. So he started a campaign to have the case reopened. A retrial couldn't bring Jean Calas back to life, but it could serve to bring out the truth.

It took Voltaire three years to force the city authorities to act; and when all the facts were brought out, the judges could do nothing but admit that Jean Calas had been innocent. His name was cleared, and his children were given their freedom from the convent and the monastery. Many Europeans were thrilled by Voltaire's work on this case, so well had he used it to dramatize the struggle against intolerance.

Through him and the other philosophers the new learning began to spread throughout Europe. But the new truths of the Enlightenment were still a closed book to the Jews. Living in ghettos in the midst of a hostile world, the Jews were sealed off from the currents of thought that were flowing through Europe. To them, the only truth worth treasuring was that found in the Talmud; the only way of life, that prescribed in the Shulchan Aruch.

Some Jews, meanwhile, were beginning to grow weary of the continuous study of the Talmud that went on in the ghettos. One of these, Israel of Moldavia, better known as Baal Shem Tob (Master of the Good Name), refused to pore for hours over the heavy tomes of the Talmud. Instead, he spent his time walking in the fields and woods. He was tired of the interminable hairsplitting arguments that occupied the rabbis and educated people of his time, the early eighteenth century. He felt the scholars were hiding the beauty of God behind clouds of words. He wanted people to *feel* and *see* God everywhere—in nature, in their thoughts, in their feelings, and in every manifestation of life on earth.

God was everywhere, said Baal Shem Tob, in the heart of the ignorant as well as the learned. Anybody's prayer, so long as it was offered with purity and fervor, was acceptable to God. The somber, mechanical rules of the Shulchan Aruch, said Shem Tob, were displeasing to God, for prayers should be joyously sung, and observances should be performed in happiness.

His followers, who were called Chasidim (the Pious Ones), joyously sang their praise of God and often broke into ecstatic dance during their services. In a world that was sad enough for the Jews outside the ghetto walls, and frequently gloomy inside, this kind of religion offered a source of satisfaction and joy. The Chasidic movement, which was limited largely to the ghettos of eastern Europe, thus brought a certain amount of gaiety and cheerfulness into the lives of the Jews. But the Chasidic movement brought the Jews not a bit closer to the intellectual ferment of Europe.

In western Europe, however, where the new knowledge was being developed. the swirling current of European thought finally penetrated the ghetto walls, for ideas respect no barriers, be they walls or policemen. In the latter half of the eighteenth century, largely as a result of the work of Moses Mendelssohn, the new learning found its way into the ghettos to create a stir among the Jews.

Moses Mendelssohn was born in Dessau, Germany, in 1729, but moved to Berlin while still a youth. There he became famous for his writings on philosophy and art. Written in graceful and fluent German, his books made him an important literary figure. He became one of the leaders in the movement to make Germans conscious of the beauty of their tongue and to get them to accept German, instead of French, as a language of culture.

Besides his books in the field of philosophy and art criticism, Mendelssohn also contributed much to the intellectual ferment of Europe by his writings on the theme of liberty, in which he stressed the need to give every individual the freedom to think and live according to his own desires. His ideas on individual liberty influenced many German Christians, among them Wilhelm Christian von Dohm, adviser to King Frederick the Great of Prussia. Mendelssohn's influence led people like von Dohm to look upon Jews as fellow human beings who deserved the same rights that were accorded Christians in Prussia.

Mendelssohn was accepted in intellectual circles of Europe as a leading advocate of German culture. The great German dramatist, Gotthold Lessing, who was an intimate friend of Mendelssohn, admired him to such an extent that he patterned the leading character of his celebrated play, *Nathan the Wise,* after Mendelssohn himself.

The Emancipation of the Jews

Although he moved in Christian circles mainly, Mendelssohn was proud of his Jewish faith. He maintained that one could assimilate the culture of the Christian world and still faithfully practice Judaism. He established a new kind of school in which courses dealing with the new learning that was current outside the ghetto walls were incorporated with the traditional Talmudic and religious studies. He translated the Pentateuch into German, adding a commentary to explain the significant ideas and passages. By studying Mendelssohn's translation, many Jews learned to read and write German, a language that was not taught in the ghettos. Armed with this language, Jews began avidly to read European classics, in German and in Hebrew translations.

Many German Jews now began to be irked by the ghetto walls. They began to feel that they belonged to Germany, not just to the ghetto. They became interested in whatever was happening in the country, and yearned for the right to mingle with their neighbors on equal terms and to take an active part in the life of the nation.

This new spirit worried the rabbis of the ghettos. They feared that the excitement of the new learning would wean Jews from their religion; that the enlightened ideas of the time would weaken the hold of the synagogue in the Jewish world, just as the new learning was weakening the authority of the Church in the Christian world.

But it wasn't the opposition of the rabbis that kept the Jews from breaking out of the ghetto mold then and there. It was the medieval attitude toward Jews, the prejudice against them that had become part of the atmosphere of Europe—that was what kept Jews within the ghettos. Although enlightened ideas were on the march, and people were moving forward, their feet seemed to become paralyzed at the gates of the ghettos. Most Europeans were simply not yet ready to regard the Jews as people like themselves, with natural rights. To them, the Jews were still a strange, alien group.

However, the bonds that held people chained to the medieval past were being loosened. In America, in 1776, the Declaration of Independence made a clean break with the Middle Ages. Jefferson's declaration, which was based on the ideas of Locke and Rousseau, aroused the people of America to sacrifice life and limb in the fight for their human rights. In Europe, particularly in France, the new ideas were also arousing the people to protest against intolerable conditions.

It was in France that Europeans first rose up in rebellion against the old system. The revolution began in 1789, when King Louis XVI, finding his royal treasury empty and fearing to tax the Church and nobility who together owned about half the land of the country, decided to raise the taxes of the common people. He sent his decree to the courts to be registered. This was a mere formality, since the courts customarily approved all royal decrees without discussion.

But these were no longer the "good old days." The ideas of the philosophers and the success of the American Revolution had convinced a lot of people that the king's mere command was no longer the law. To the astonishment of Louis and his noblemen, the judges refused to accept the tax decree, on the ground that only the people had the right to approve the laws of the government. The

philosophers had put words in their mouths! Get the con-
sent of the governed, they told Louis.

No threats of the exasperated king could move the
judges, and Louis was forced to call a meeting of the representatives of the clergy, the nobility, and the common people. The king regarded the meeting as a nuisance—an unnecessary one at that. Since each class—the nobility, the
clergy, and the common people—voted as a group, each
casting one vote, Louis thought it a foregone conclusion
that the nobility and clergy, voting together, would adopt
the new tax schedules.

But to the common people of France the meeting in
1789 was not a silly business at all. It was an opportunity
they had been waiting for. The peasants complained about
having to pay the lords rent for land they felt was really
theirs, and demanded an end to the feudal services the
lords had forced upon them in ancient days. The shop-
keepers and professionals of the towns objected to being
treated as inferiors, and demanded the same rights enjoyed
by the lords and the clergy.

Inspired by the Declaration of Independence which had
been issued thirteen years before in America, the leaders
of the common people insisted that no one group should
have rights that the others did not enjoy. "Equal rights for
all," they said, and no more voting according to classes.

Then word came that King Louis was planning to break
up the meeting. The people sprang to action. In Paris they
stormed the Bastille, an ancient royal prison; and in the
villages, the peasants marched against their lords, forcing
them to give up the deeds and contracts which listed the
feudal dues owed by the peasants.

The meeting King Louis had called to rubber-stamp his decree was transformed into a sort of Congress, a National Assembly. It abolished the special privileges of the nobility and clergy, and declared everyone equal before the law— no more special courts or special laws for any class. Feudal dues were abolished. Citizens were guaranteed freedom of religion and speech, and freedom from arbitrary arrest and imprisonment. Later the National Assembly deposed the king and established a Republic.

When it came to the question of giving the Jews the rights reserved for Frenchmen, the leaders did not flinch. The Catholic priest, Abbé Grégoire, who sided with the people, denounced the persecutions and attacks that Jews had suffered in France. Count Clermont-Tonnerre, an aristocrat who also sided with the people, declared that Christian society had committed many sins against the Jews in the past, and it was now high time to atone for them. Some members of the Assembly did hesitate. They were not prepared to accept Jews as equal members of the national family. But the new spirit could not be denied; and on November 13, 1791, the resolution to include the Jews as equal citizens was passed. The new laws guaranteed to all people, no matter what their religion, the right to enter any occupation they wanted to, and Protestants and Jews were given equal rights with Catholics to hold office in the government.

The French Revolution turned its back on the Middle Ages; it made the common man and the Jew human beings, persons of dignity and importance. But the aristocracy and the leaders of the Church looked back with longing to the "good old days" when people were more ignorant and superstitious; when people had not dared to demand rights or question the doctrines the upper classes chose to teach them. Small wonder, then, that the privileged groups of Europe declared war on the French Revolution!

At this the people of France rose up in arms to defend their new constitution and their hard-won rights. The Jews of France joined the struggle heartily. Many enlisted in the army, while congregations donated the treasures of their synagogues to help the war effort. The synagogues themselves rang out with prayers for victory, for the French Revolution had brought them freedom and the right to live and work as human beings, as citizens of the French nation.

For many years the war to save the Revolution raged. When Napoleon took over the leadership of the government, the French armies began a victorious march through Europe. To the Jews in their path, their arrival meant an opportunity to breathe the new air of freedom. Wherever the French armies conquered, the walls of the ghetto fell and the Jews walked free. And when Napoleon took Spain, the hated Inquisition was abolished. The air of Europe seemed to be clearing as the fresh winds blew in from France. The common man lifted up his head. So did the Jew, and he held out his hand in fellowship to his Christian neighbor.

Many Christians were prepared to accept the Jews as neighbors. Like Wilhelm von Dohm, they were able to think about them without hostile emotions. Von Dohm, in a report to King Frederick the Great, showed that the various criticisms people made against Jews—that they were clannish, wore peculiar clothes, and engaged mostly in peddling and moneylending—all these characteristics of their life, he pointed out, had actually been forced on them by anti-Jewish laws. Let the king abolish these laws, he said. Let him give them the same opportunities for work and education, permit them to live like their neighbors, and the Jews would develop the same ideas, customs, and loyalties his other subjects had.

Even before the Revolution, many Christians had become emancipated from the medieval attitude toward Jews. The French philosopher, Montesquieu, early in the eighteenth century, had branded Europeans as barbarians for their treatment of Jews. And in 1782, Joseph II of Austria, had issued the Edict of Toleration abolishing the special body tax collected from Jews, as well as the insulting requirement that they wear beards and specified articles of clothing. The law also permitted Jews to move about a little more freely in his realm.

But these well-meaning Christians were comparatively few; they were vastly outnumbered by those who had blind spots when it came to Jews. Scholars who had freed themselves from the chains of medieval beliefs somehow left part of their minds in the Middle Ages whenever they thought of Jews. Even such thinkers as Goethe, the noted German poet, and Fichte, the German historian: one called the Jews inferior and the other pronounced them unworthy of German citizenship. The great Voltaire, himself, was not entirely free of anti-Jewish prejudice. As a result of some business deal through a Jewish agent, he lost some money, and claimed that the Jew had tricked him. In an article he wrote shortly afterward, he attacked the Jews as a selfish people, greedy for money!

The Emancipation of the Jews

There is some question as to whether he had actually been tricked, but that isn't important. What did matter was that the great enemy of intolerance saw fit to attack all Jews for an alleged crime committed by one of them. True, when friends reminded Voltaire that he had been guilty of the very thing against which he had been battling all his life, he did apologize for "attributing to a whole nation the faults of some of them." But not all Christians were that broadminded. All too many of them found it easier to lump Jews together and to think of them all in unfriendly terms.

For most Europeans of that time, the prejudices of the past had greater force than logical reasoning. The word "Jew" had come down as a term almost synonymous with "enemy," someone a Christian had to be wary of. They still believed, because people they respected were still teaching it to them, that Jews killed Jesus and that they murdered Christian children so they could use their blood in the Passover rituals. And they were still being told that the Jews were a "different" people who just "didn't belong."

The soldiers of revolutionary France, however, brushed aside all prejudices. To them, all men were equal, and they were not inclined to argue about it. Free the serfs, throw open the ghetto gates—long live liberty, equality, brotherhood! But in 1815 France fell, defeated by the combined armies of the nobility of Europe; and the aristocrats again took power.

The ruling class determined to return to the old order, to put the common people back in their place. They made war against all ideas that favored liberty and the people's rights. They began to rule with an iron hand and suppressed, as much as they could, all activities in behalf of the common man.

Although it was now the nineteenth century, it seemed that the Middle Ages were actually about to return. Everywhere in Europe, the common man lost much that he had gained from the Revolution, and so did the Jews. Ghettos were re-established in many countries. In some ghettos the Jews had again to listen in their synagogues at least once a year to a special conversion sermon preached by a priest. The Inquisition came back to life in Spain and Italy, and laws restricting the life and work of Jews were re-enacted. Many states set quotas on the number of Jewish families permitted within their borders.

By the nineteenth century, however, Europeans had begun to think differently from their medieval ancestors. The common people had no desire to go back to the "good old days" when they had had no say in the government; when they had been regarded by the nobility as a lower class. Especially irritated were the newly-risen industrialists, whose factories were producing the wealth of the various nations. They demanded their full share in the government so they could get laws more favorable to business. They did not like the policies of the landed aristocracy who controlled the governments after 1815.

The workers also demanded a voice in the government; not simply because they wanted equal rights as human beings, but particularly because they wanted laws to improve the conditions under which they lived and worked. Their unions and political parties began to clamor for shorter hours and better pay, for laws to clean up the unsanitary factories in which people worked and the slums in which they lived.

The aristocrats paid little attention to the demands of these groups, just as they disregarded the interests of the landless peasants on their estates. The people finally rose up in rebellion in the years 1830 and 1848; the revolutions tumbled a number of kings from their thrones. And those kings who did keep their thrones were forced to accept constitutions that gave many of the common people the right to vote. Special privileges for the aristocrats were abolished, feudal dues and services were ended, and the civil rights of the people were officially recognized.

The year of revolution, 1848, was not the year of the millennium; it did not solve all the problems that afflicted the people. It did not assure everyone an adequate income so he could enjoy more of the good things of life. Far from it! But it was a sign that Europe was moving forward toward liberty, equality, and security.

Many Jews took part in this movement. They realized that their right to live as Jews would never be completely secure under the old autocratic system and that freedom for them depended upon the spread of democracy for *all* people. In the countries of western Europe, where most of the revolutions took place, the Jews asked for no special privileges for themselves as Jews. I. N. Mannheimer, a Jew who was one of the leaders of the revolt in Austria, expressed the feeling of most Jews when he said, "For us, nothing! Everything for people and country. First the right to live as a man—to breathe, to think, to speak. First the right of the citizen—the Jew comes afterwards!"

In Germany as in Austria and elsewhere, many Jews took

part in the march of the common man, even becoming leaders in the liberal movement. One such leader, Karl Ludwig Börne, from the ghetto of Frankfort, who resented the fact that Jews were compelled to walk in the gutters of the city simply because they were Jews, joined the "Young Germany" movement to work for a more democratic Germany. The government censor banned his writings on the subject of liberty, branding them as dangerous. But Börne's articles were secretly circulated throughout the country, and they helped to make the "Young Germany" movement grow. Another Jewish leader of this democratic party was Heinrich Heine, one of the greatest poets produced by Germany, whose passionate poems on liberty inspired many to work for a free and united Germany.

In many countries the revolutionary leaders included emancipation for the Jews as part of their program. Many Christians actually began to regard the confinement of Jews to ghettos as a symbol of medieval autocracy. In Italy, for instance, one of Mazzini's followers, Alfredo Brunetti, brought six thousand Italian citizens into the Roman ghetto one day in 1847 where they enthusiastically fraternized with the Jews, and promised them to work for their social and political emancipation. And the following year, on April 17, 1848, when public announcement was made by the papal authorities that the Roman ghetto would be abolished, Brunetti rounded up many of his friends and immediately set to work to tear the walls down.

The Jews of western Europe were being freed from the ghettos, and they were winning citizenship rights. Many medieval restrictions were abolished, and they were able to move about and live like other free men. It was the dawn of a new day in Europe for all people; Jews, as well as Christians who had suffered under autocracy, could greet the new day with hope. For, as the common man achieved his rights as a human being, the Jew, fighting alongside him as a fellow human, went forward with him. The spirit of democracy, first voiced by the Prophets of Israel so many centuries before, was beginning to take root in Christian Europe.

CHAPTER THIRTEEN

Jews East and Jews West

$\mathcal{I}$N the years following the revolutions of 1848, the Jews of western Europe won many rights, not the least of which was the right to live wherever they wanted to. They mingled with their Christian neighbors at school, at work, and in their leisure hours. They became integrated into the life of the peoples among whom they lived. And they were proud that they "belonged," that they were part of the national family.

It was an exciting feeling. For many generations they had been shut off from the Christian world, forced to think of themselves only as Jews, as outsiders. Their neighbors in those days spoke the language of the country, while the Jews in most of the ghettos considered Yiddish as their mother tongue. But now, going to the same schools as the others, reading the same books, they began to accept German, English, or Italian—whatever languages were spoken in the countries in which they lived—as their native tongue.

Yes, it was a grand thing to be a citizen! And the vast

majority of Jews took their citizenship seriously. But they were not completely accepted in all respects as part of the national family. Since many governments regarded their countries as Christian states, some of them still recognizing Christianity, Catholic or Protestant, as the official religion of the land, only Christians were permitted to teach in the schools and universities. Nor could Jews hold government positions in many countries. A person elected to Parliament in England, for instance, was required to swear to uphold the constitution on his "true faith as a Christian." And England was one of the more enlightened countries, too!

In spite of this "Christian" oath, Lionel Rothschild, a Jew, ran for Parliament in 1847 and was elected. When he appeared in the House of Commons to be sworn in, he refused to take the oath because his true faith was Judaism. Nevertheless, he demanded that he be admitted as a member, since he had been elected by the free vote of the people.

If any Jew had made such demands a hundred years earlier, he would have been laughed at or treated roughly. Instead, many Christians now joined with Rothschild in a campaign to have the law changed. The famous historian, Thomas B. Macaulay, attacked the oath as being against the whole democratic spirit of the times. There were many years of arguing, but the law was finally changed in 1858. Rothschild was admitted to the House of Commons, and from that time on, Jews could become members of Parliament.

In the same year, 1858, another incident took place that put to the test the new spirit in Europe. On the night of June 26 of that year, police came to the door of the Mortara family in the city of Bologna, Italy. They demanded in the name of the Pope that little six-year-old Edgar Mortara be handed over to them. Mr. Mortara couldn't understand why the police should want Edgar. Had the little boy committed a crime? They had orders, said the police, to deliver Edgar Mortara to a Catholic school, where he was to be brought up as a Catholic. "But there must be some mistake," said the stunned father, "for we are Jews." The police shook their heads. There was no mistake at all. And they showed him a baptismal certificate made out in the name of Edgar Mortara.

The parents were speechless. They had never baptized Edgar and had no wish for him to be brought up as a Catholic. The police weren't interested. They had their orders and took the boy away.

Frantic, the parents went to the authorities to plead for the return of their son. From them they learned that Edgar had been secretly baptized by his Catholic nursemaid some years before. The officials were sympathetic, but once a child was baptized, he belonged to the Church. There was nothing that could be done about it.

The Jewish community appealed to the sense of justice and fair play of Christians all over Europe, urging them to ask the Pope to have Edgar returned to his parents.

Sir Moses Montefiore, a famous English Jew, made a special trip to Rome, but the Pope refused to see him. Emperors Francis Joseph of Austria and Napoleon III of France, both Catholics, sent word to the Pope suggesting he undo the wrong done the Mortaras. In England and other countries public meetings and demonstrations were held to protest against the medieval action of the Church authorities. But the Pope refused to release the child. It was reported that the Pope, Pius IX, said he "snapped his fingers" at all the protests and appeals. The Jewish community was even warned by some Church officials to drop the whole matter, or else life would become unbearable for them in the Papal States. The Jews refused to be silenced. They continued to protest. But in spite of all the pressure, Edgar Mortara was not released. Reared as a Catholic, he later became a priest.

Although the case was lost, it did show that nineteenth century Europe was different from the Europe of the Middle Ages. Had the incident occurred in the 1500's, very few Christians would have been aroused or even disturbed. The Jews themselves would probably have hesitated to protest. But people in the nineteenth century seemed to be more willing to speak out in the name of decency and fair play, even though it meant criticism of the Church.

In many other ways, the nineteenth century was an era of great achievement. There were many inventions and discoveries: the telegraph, the telephone, the steamship, and the railroad were making the world seem a different place from what it had been. So much was being done, so much work and thought and planning were going on, that anyone who had ideas, who could offer muscle or brain to keep the wheels of progress turning, was welcome. The world itself seemed to be on the move.

In the Middle Ages there had been little movement. From one generation to another, life had gone on pretty much in the same pattern. In fact, the rulers—the kings, the lords, and the Church—were against change, against new ways and new ideas. Their power would be unquestioned so long as people conformed to the pattern—so long as they believed alike, thought alike, and accepted things as they were.

But in the nineteenth century it was the business interests that controlled the governments and shaped their policies. And what businessmen wanted most from their country was that trade and manufacturing should be profitable. Conformity in religion was not too important to them, for business profited from the work a man did, not from his beliefs. In such an atmosphere it became easier for a Jew to enter into the life and work of his country.

Formerly in the ghettos, Jews of ability had devoted their energies to the few occupations in which the laws permitted them to engage, and their minds were occupied almost exclusively with Jewish studies. Now, in the emancipated areas of Europe, they began to express their talents in business, the arts, medicine, science, and all other fields to which they were admitted. In such a world Elisa Felix Rachel of France could reach great heights as an actress; Ernesto Nathan could be elected mayor of Rome; Nathaniel Mayer Rothschild could be raised to the peerage by Queen Victoria; Luigi Luzzatti could become a member of the cabinet of the national government of Italy.

The day of complete equality and brotherhood, the day of the Prophetic dream, however, had not yet arrived. The deep-seated prejudices of the Middle Ages did not disappear so readily. In Switzerland, for instance, Jews were still permitted to live only in certain areas, even after the revolution of 1848, and very few of them were allowed to attend the universities. But no longer did they have to fight alone for their rights, for Christians within Switzerland joined them. Help came, too, from the government of

France. The Swiss government had signed a treaty permitting French citizens to own land in Switzerland. Since French Jews were denied that right in the Swiss city of Berne, the French government protested it; it objected to the Swiss government's dividing Frenchmen into Christians and Jews, and denying to the French Jews rights they granted the French Christians. Finally in 1873, Switzerland gave the Jews complete equality.

It must have been a wonderful feeling for the Jews of France to know that they were considered a real part of the French nation, and that their country was ready to protect them. It made them happy to be accepted as Frenchmen, and they developed a deep sense of loyalty to the state. Not only in France, but throughout western Europe most Jews began to look upon themselves as citizens first—Frenchmen, Germans, Austrians, Dutch, English— and Jews afterward. The Jews of western Europe were losing their ghetto idea of being a people apart.

The only thing, they felt, that made them in any way different from their neighbors was their religion. They went to synagogue on Saturday; others went to church on Sunday. Aside from religious beliefs and observances in synagogue and home, there was nothing to distinguish them from the others, for they were no longer forced by law to live separately, under their own rules, following a distinctively Jewish pattern of life. Now they chose of their own free will to live like their neighbors.

This did not mean that they lost interest in things Jewish. In fact, there developed a new sense of pride in the past history and achievements of the Jews. Many Jewish scholars, particularly in Germany and England, made the study of Jewish history their specialty, and brought to light, from neglected books and records, facts heretofore unknown about Jewish life. Their studies showed that Jews, both as individuals and as a people, had contributed a great deal toward the growth and development of European civilization.

All of this great literature caused the Jews of western Europe to hold their heads high, to feel proud of their ancestry. Books about the Jewish past, like Graetz's great *History of the Jews* also helped to acquaint many Christians with the real story of the Jewish people. Most Europeans had very queer notions of what a Jew was, and knew next to nothing of his history. Bit by bit, more exact knowledge about the Jews and their religion began to spread through the western countries, with the result that Jews became more and more accepted as real parts of the various national families.

In eastern Europe the Jews underwent an entirely different development. While western Europe was gradually becoming more democratic, eastern Europe still lived under the feudalism of the Middle Ages. The common people of eastern Europe were either serfs or peasants, practically slaves on the estates where they lived and worked.

Their rulers governed them with great strictness and deliberately kept them ignorant and superstitious. Catherine the Great of Russia once said in a letter to a nobleman, "The day when our peasants shall wish to become enlightened, both you and I will lose our places." Deep down, the nobles and kings feared the serfs and peasants, for they had made them into work horses. In fact, horses in Russia were better off than the people—at least the horses were curried and cleaned, fed regularly and given stalls to sleep in. No such careful attention was paid to the serfs. Their lot was but to work and obey, and be thankful that they were alive.

The fifty million Russian peasants of the early nineteenth century were kept in bondage and obedience by special police and soldiers. No criticism of the czar or the nobility was allowed. The rulers did not want the peasants to start demanding their human rights as the common man in western Europe was doing.

Religion was also used as a weapon of suppression. In Russia, the czar was the head of the Church, and the priests taught the people to look upon him as a god, their "Little White Father." They were also taught that it was a virtue to be patient and uncomplaining, since all would be well for them in the next world. It was profitable for the czar and the nobility to keep the peasants feeling that way, for it meant they would have plenty of labor at extremely low wages.

If the rulers took such advantage of their fellow Christians, imagine what their attitude must have been toward the Jews! Not only were the Jews of a different religion, but most of them were not even Russians. The majority of them lived in Poland, which was then only a province within the Russian Empire.

The czars specified certain districts in Poland and White Russia as places where Jews were permitted to live. This area came to be known as the "Pale of Settlement." It was simply an enlarged ghetto for some two million Jews. The czars treated the Poles and other non-Russian groups badly, but the Jews fared even worse. The laws for them were harsher, particularly in the matter of military service. By the Conscription Law of 1827, Jews were forced to serve for a term of twenty-five years. For every thousand Jews in a community, ten children had to be provided for the army, and the heads of each community were held responsible for the delivery of the required number.

That was quite a distasteful job for the Jews. Naturally, no parent wanted his child to be chosen, particularly since it was the policy of the government to try to convert the Jewish youths to Christianity during their term of service. But since the burden was on the community to recruit the children, ways had to be found for getting them. Children of Jews who had no passports to settle in a particular town were seized by the recruiting committee. Orphans, or children from poor families, were often torn from their mothers' arms and carried away by force. In many Jewish towns men were hired actually to kidnap children for the army.

Besides the nightmare of having to recruit children, the czar's government visited other sufferings upon the Jews. In 1835 the Pale of Settlement was reduced in size, thus forcing the Jews to crowd together into smaller areas. On top of that, they were forbidden to enter certain towns and villages where they had been accustomed to carry on business. There were so few opportunities for work left to them that it became almost impossible for most of the Jews to earn a living.

In fact, in the year 1843, in the Polish part of the Russian Empire only about one out of every ten Jews had a job that paid him enough to support his family. The other ninety per cent were so poverty-stricken they had to depend upon outside help to make ends meet. Nor were the Jews much better off in Russia proper.

Christian serfs and peasants also suffered, but at least they were safe from attack. The Jews were not. Often, when the government saw the peasants becoming angry and discontented, the officials circulated ugly rumors and stories about Jews, and had hostile sermons preached against them in the churches, in order to make the peasants believe that the Jews were responsible for their suffering. When the peasants were sufficiently aroused, the agents of the government provoked them into making brutal attacks upon the Jewish community. These pogroms, as they were called, not only brought death and anguish to the Jews, but also fixed the idea pretty firmly in the minds of the peasants that it was the Jews, not their rulers, who were to blame for their hardships.

But neither through pogroms nor special police could the government build a wall high enough to keep out the revolutionary ideas that came into Russia from the West as if borne on the breeze. Intelligent Russians, disturbed by the bad conditions in the country and irritated by the autocratic activities of the government, organized a number of societies to seek reforms in the country. They circulated books and pamphlets attacking the czar, the Church, and the nobility. The common people of Russia soon began to hear a lot about the Rights of Man.

In the 1850's, meanwhile, the czar became involved in the Crimean War, a bloody war which Russia lost. After the war the peasants found conditions so intolerable that they rebelled on a number of estates, demanding land of their own and freedom from the oppression of the nobles.

Czar Alexander II feared a revolution of the kind that had occurred in western Europe, where a number of kings had lost their thrones. To prevent it, he decided in 1861 to free the serfs, permitting some to leave the estates to which they had been bound, and providing others with land from the very estates on which they had been held in serfdom.

The czar did not do this out of the goodness of his heart, but because the Crimean War had shown that Russia was quite backward in comparison with the West. He felt that Russia would never be strong economically or in war unless it had industry on a large scale, as they had it in western Europe. But most of the manpower of Russia—the serfs and peasants—was on the great estates, where the laws of Russia had kept them like prisoners. The emancipation of the serfs made it possible to move some of them to the cities where their labor was needed for the factories and railroads that were being built.

The need for workers to industrialize Russia could not be met by the freeing of the serfs alone. A great many of the peasants were still needed to work on the farms. So the czar turned to the Jews. He gave them the privilege of living anywhere in the empire, if they were engaged in commerce or industry, thus freeing them from the Pale of Settlement. This led a great many Jews to enter trades and to become skilled workers. Many left for the larger cities, where they opened small shops in their homes. Some of the shops grew until they actually became factories. Other Jews became merchants or storekeepers.

Jews began to spread out into various parts of the Russian Empire—not only the workers, but also educated Jews, for the new laws also permitted Jews with university or college degrees to settle anywhere in the country. Most of the Jews, however, were artisans—tailors, shoemakers, blacksmiths, and so forth—for there was a great demand for such workers in the early days of the industrial growth of Russia.

This new opportunity to earn a livelihood was not an unmixed blessing, however; for the workers, both Christian and Jewish, received little pay for long hours of labor. When the workers started to organize unions to increase their wages and to improve conditions of work, the police were ordered to break up the unions. The czar was interested in protecting the profits of industry. The unions therefore became secret, underground organizations. Opposition to the government increased to such an extent that it took the form of violence and terrorism. The bombing of government buildings and assassination of officials became common occurrences. In 1881, Czar Alexander II himself was assassinated.

The new czar, Alexander III, in retaliation, made Russia practically a prison. Everything and everybody was watched. By the trainloads people were exiled to Siberia for daring to criticize conditions in the country. Many Russians left the country, to seek freedom and opportunity elsewhere.

For the Jews life became hard indeed. Special decrees, known as the May Laws, issued in 1882, denied them the right to own or rent land in rural areas. They were driven out of Moscow and other cities in which they had settled. Jewish workers lost their jobs, and merchants their businesses. New ghetto districts were established, and the right of Jews to travel about the country was strictly limited.

In many ways they were made to feel they were unwelcome strangers in the land they had lived in for generations. Pogroms increased in number and intensity, and Jews by the thousands began to leave the country. Most of them came to America. Others went to Germany, to England, to the Argentine, to South Africa; anywhere, just to get away from the hopeless life in Russia.

The vast majority of Jews, of course, remained in Russia. Some had business interests that kept them there; but most of them simply had no money to take them elsewhere. Many were content, for religious reasons, to live in their Jewish communities, where they could continue the customs and traditions of Judaism. Indeed, there were quite a few Jews who did not mind remaining in Russia, but they wanted more out of life than the cramped existence the ghettos offered them. They were eager to become a part of Russia, just as the Jews of western Europe had become citizens of their native lands. They wanted to be accepted as equals in Russia.

These ideas had been introduced into eastern Jewish life through a literary movement called *Haskalah*, a Hebrew word meaning "enlightenment." For a long time a Jew had been considered educated if he were expert in the Talmud. But the writers of the Haskalah, who were influenced by the ideas of Moses Mendelssohn, wanted the Jews to widen their knowledge, to become enlightened through acquaintance with the new learning that was spreading throughout Europe.

One of the early writers of the Haskalah, Isaac Ber Levinsohn, in his book *Learning in Israel*, written in 1828, pointed out that Jewish thought as represented by the

Bible and the Talmud was fine as far as it went, but it had
to be added to because the world had made great advances
in art, science, and philosophy since Talmudic times. If
Jews were to participate in Russian life on a basis of
equality, then they must become acquainted with the culture not only of Russia, but of Europe as well. Jewish writers then translated into Yiddish and Hebrew many of the
books that the rest of the world was reading. They also
started magazines and papers that dealt with Jewish history
and philosophy, as well as with the literature and drama
that was being produced in other countries.

The Haskalah movement gave the Jews the sense of
belonging to an ancient, honorable people. But it did not
lead them to feel they were part of the national family of
Russia, as the Jews of the West felt in their countries. The
countries of eastern Europe, unlike the nations of the West,
were made up of many different peoples. Poland, for instance, was part of the Russian Empire. But the people
living there considered themselves as Poles, not Russians.
In the nineteenth century there was no Czechoslovakia. It
was a province of the Austro-Hungarian Empire. The people of the area thought of themselves as Czechs, not Austrians or Hungarians.

Many of the peoples in eastern Europe, moreover, had
once been independent nations, before they had been conquered. There were many such submerged peoples in
eastern Europe who continued to live on the same land
they had always occupied, land which they regarded as
their national home; they continued to speak their native
tongue, and to observe the customs and folkways they had
developed during the centuries they had lived together as

independent nations. Their customs, language, and even their religion were often as different from those of the ruling nation as the Poles, for instance, were different from the Russians in those respects.

The eastern European peoples were generally proud of their past history and accomplishments, and wanted to continue their ancient folkways. They were angry and resentful when their new (and to them, foreign) rulers tried to force them to give up their way of life and become like their conquerors, for they saw no good reason to give up what was so natural and meaningful to them, just because they had new rulers. Peoples like the Czechs and Poles insisted on retaining their national cultures; they lived as "nations within a nation."

The Haskalah movement developed a similar national feeling among the Jews of eastern Europe. They, too, had their own languages, Yiddish and Hebrew, tongues that were different from their rulers'. They, too, had ancient folkways and a culture peculiar to themselves, for the Jews had developed a special way of life based on the festivals, holidays, and the laws of the Talmud. They felt that they also, in a sense, had a "native homeland"—the Pale of Settlement. They had lived in those areas for many generations as if in a separate country, for they had their own local governments in their communities, with the power of making rules and regulations for the Jews of the Pale. And they had built out of their years of living together there, a literature and a culture that was distinctly their own, a Jewish culture.

Eastern and western Europe developed different ideas of citizenship. In western Europe the Enlightenment freed the individual; he was no longer simply identified as a member of some social class, but a human being with civil and political rights of his own. He was a citizen of his country by virtue of his residence in it, having the same legal rights as other residents. When the Jews of western lands were emancipated from the ghettos, they too became equal citizens; they adopted the national language as their own and entered into the political and economic life of the nation equally with the other citizens. To all practical purpose, they were distinguished from their fellow citizens only in religion, just as Catholics and Protestants were different from other citizens by virtue of their religion.

In the East, where various small nations had been forcefully incorporated into empires and treated as subject nations, the submerged national groups became minority nations—nations within a nation. Their members were not regarded as equals by the ruling nation. The individual member of the minority nation was not considered a citizen of the ruling nation.

The Jews of eastern Europe reacted the way the other minority peoples did. Like the others, they refused to give up their religion and language, in which so much of their history and literature was written, and resented being treated like subject foreigners by the government. Like the other minorities, the Jews felt themselves to be a distinct people with a way of life that was their very own.

Some Jewish writers, like Perez Smolenskin and Leon Pinsker, even urged the Jews to think of themselves as a nation, not simply people who were bound together by religious customs. If people were Jews only because of their religious beliefs, then the Jews who no longer accepted the traditional beliefs of the Jewish religion should not be called Jews. But they *were* called Jews, and they themselves *wanted* to be known as Jews. They had done so many things together for such a long time that they were a definite nationality, said Smolenskin and Pinsker; all they needed was a homeland and a government of their own to make them a nation.

The feeling of Jewish nationhood became strong especially toward the end of the century, when life became extremely difficult for the Jews in Russia, Romania, and the other lands of eastern Europe. Many eastern Jews began to think their only hope for security lay in the establishment of an independent Jewish nation somewhere, perhaps in Palestine, with which region so much Jewish history and religion was associated.

Up to the middle of the nineteenth century the eastern and western European Jewish communities were the main centers of Jewish life. By the end of the century, however, the Jews of the United States had increased in numbers to such an extent as to become a vital factor in Jewish life. The experience of the Jews in this country differed considerably from that of the Jews of eastern and western Europe. The Jews of America therefore developed a quite different outlook.

In Europe the Jews had been for many centuries physically separated from their neighbors by the ghetto. It was during the ghetto centuries that the peoples of western Europe developed a national feeling. When the Jews of western Europe were emancipated, therefore, they had to go through a period of adjustment before they were integrated and accepted into the national family. In eastern

Europe, where they did not achieve actual emancipation, instead of being integrated into the national scene they developed the same outlook as did other minority nationalities.

In America, however, the Jews did not start out as strangers, as new residents in a long-established country. They came in the early colonial period, when all the early settlers were also immigrants in a new land. They were not compelled to live as a separate community, off by themselves in ghettos, but right from the start, they lived and worked alongside the other settlers.

The first Jews who came in a group to North America arrived in 1654. Actually, the Jews had been connected with the New World before then. The improvements in the compass made by Jewish geographers and scientists, and their work in the field of navigation, helped make it possible for Columbus to plan his explorations. The money that furnished Columbus with ships and supplies came largely from Marranos, the secret Jews in the court of Ferdinand and Isabella. And included in Columbus' crew in 1492 were five or six Jews. But the first Jews to settle permanently in the United States were the twenty-three who came to New Amsterdam, in the days when that Dutch colony was governed by Peter Stuyvesant.

The same reason that caused the Pilgrims to migrate to the New World in 1620 drove those Jews from Brazil to New Amsterdam in 1654. Up to that year, Brazil had been a Dutch colony and Jews were permitted to settle there. Many Jews had come to Brazil to live and work and enjoy religious liberty, a rare privilege in those days. But the Portuguese conquered Brazil in 1654 and established the

Inquisition there. To remain in Brazil, the Jews would have had to become Catholics. Instead they chose to flee to Holland and other parts of Europe. Twenty-three came to New Amsterdam.

But this handful of Jews met no welcome from Peter Stuyvesant. He was a European who had brought to America the prejudices he had developed in the Old World. If he had had his way, he would have refused to allow this little band of Jews to enter the colony. But the directors of the Dutch West India Company, which owned the colony, ordered him to let the Jews remain. It didn't seem right to bar Jews from New Amsterdam when they were welcome in old Amsterdam, in Holland. So Stuyvesant was instructed to give the Jews the same rights the other settlers in the colony enjoyed.

When their right to remain had been established, the Jews took it for granted that they were part of the Dutch "family." They presented themselves to the council to be assigned their places in the guard, since all males were required to do guard duty because of the danger of attack by unfriendly Indians or other enemies. But Stuyvesant had a special law passed to keep the Jews out of the guard. They were ordered to pay a tax instead.

The Jews did not want exemptions from their duties. They demanded the right to help protect the colony like the others. They protested to Holland that Stuyvesant was not treating them as equals in the community. Asser Levy, the leader of the Jewish group, did not wait for the reply to come from Holland. He took his turn standing guard without official permission. When the reply came that the Jews were legitimate settlers, not a special group within

New Amsterdam, Stuyvesant was forced to grant the Jews complete citizenship, which he did in 1657.

At that very time, the Jews of Europe were living in ghettos. They did not dare to make demands. But the Jews of New Amsterdam were living in a different world. There were no "old timers" there, whose families had lived in the land for generations, and who were suspicious of newcomers lest they interfere with their comfort or prosperity. They were all "immigrants." There were Protestant refugees from Catholic Belgium and France; Catholics and Puritans from England; Lutherans and Anabaptists from Germany; and Jews from Brazil and Europe. As a matter of fact, there were more than fifteen languages spoken in New Amsterdam alone. Jews, therefore, didn't stand out as particularly different from the rest.

Everybody in early America had to work together, to build and defend their communities. Since the settlers were so dependent on one another, they were more ready to help each other, and the Jews entered into the spirit of things. Asser Levy, for instance, lent money to the Lutherans so they could build their first church in New York.

From Central and South America, from Europe and elsewhere a trickle of Jews came to America. Most of them were descendants of the expelled Spanish and Portuguese Jews. From 1655 on, Rhode Island attracted many of them, because the founder of the colony, Roger Williams, made it a refuge for all religious groups. The first synagogue in America was organized in 1658 in Newport, Rhode Island. Jews also settled in South Carolina, Georgia, and Pennsylvania.

The Jews, like other Americans, made their way westward—to pioneer in what was then called the wilderness. Meyer Hart and his wife were among the forty people who established the town of Easton, in the frontier area of Pennsylvania. The records show that Hart contributed to the building of the first free public school in that community in 1753. And as America expanded further westward, many Jews became pioneers along with others who were migrating toward Cincinnati and Chicago. Some towns on the way were actually named after Jewish settlers, like Franks Town, Aaronsburgh, and Gratzburg.

By the time of the American Revolution, there were about two thousand Jews out of a total population of some three million. Most of them were merchants; some were farmers, artisans, or other types of workers. They entered those fields for the same reason other Americans did: they were honest ways of making a living.

The Jews developed the same feelings and ideas as their neighbors. When the American colonists objected to the interference of the British government with their freedom in trade and manufacturing, Jews were among the objectors. When American merchants signed agreements to boycott British goods, many Jewish merchants were among the signers. And when Americans organized "The Sons of Liberty" to arouse the country to the need for American independence, a number of Jews also joined this organization.

A very active member of the Sons of Liberty was Haym Salomon, who had come to America from Poland. In that country he had been a follower of Kosciusko and Pulaski, in the fight against the autocratic rulers of Poland. Like Kosciusko and Pulaski, who came to America to help Washington and the American people win their battle for freedom, Salomon also came to America when Poland lost its independence.

During the American Revolution, the British conquered New York, and arrested Haym Salomon because of his revolutionary activities. Since he knew many languages, he was not kept in prison, but was used as an interpreter among the European soldiers the British had hired to fight for them in America. On the sly, Salomon persuaded many of these to desert the British and to join Washington.

In August, 1778, he was sentenced to be hanged, for the British had found out that he had been helping American spies and aiding American prisoners to escape, and that he had been keeping in touch with Washington's army. The night before the scheduled hanging Salomon managed to escape, and made his way to Philadelphia. There, he helped Robert Morris, the treasurer for the thirteen colonies, raise money to carry on the war. The records show that Salomon gave or lent hundreds of thousands of dollars of his own funds to help the revolutionary cause. He often laid out money to pay the salaries of government officials, when the treasury had no funds, so that they could go on with their work. James Madison, James Monroe, Kosciusko, Edmund Randolph, and others were helped by Salomon in this way. And he refused to take any interest on such loans, feeling that interest should be charged only when the borrower was going to use the money for business purposes.

Besides Salomon, many other Jews took a very active part in the Revolution. Quite a number of them served in the army, both as officers and enlisted men. Many of them, like

Benjamin Nones, were promoted to officerships because of their courage and bravery under fire.

There were some Americans, however—about one-third of the colonists—who opposed the Revolution. Most of these Tories, as they were called, were of the wealthy class. There were a few Jews among this group, too. But the vast majority of the Jews were wholeheartedly on the side of Washington.

The Jews, throughout the colonial period, had enjoyed complete equality and religious freedom in most of the states. In a few states, however, the medieval sickness of religious prejudice that had been brought over to America from Europe still existed. In such states, Jews were not permitted to hold certain government positions. In some, Catholics were also denied this right.

Led by Rabbi Gershom Mendez Seixas, Haym Salomon, and others, the Jews protested against this undemocratic discrimination, pointing out that it was unfair to the many Jews who had fought to make America free. As a result, the constitution of Pennsylvania was changed in 1790 so that Jews and others could hold office, regardless of their religious beliefs and practices. The law in Virginia was also changed, after Thomas Jefferson attacked religious prejudice as being against the whole spirit of the Declaration of Independence and the Revolution. In Maryland, Thomas Kennedy, a member of Jefferson's political party, successfully fought to abolish the undemocratic oath required of state legislators; it was removed in 1818. This particular oath—"on my true faith as a Christian"—was similar to the one against which Rothschild had to fight some forty years later in England.

There were really very few restrictions against Jews in the early days of our history. They were not forced to feel they were a special people, apart from the others. From the beginning they were Americans; and side by side with Americans of all faiths they worked to develop the nation and to promote its ideals.

Even the experiences of the Jews in ancient times exerted a profound influence upon the thoughts and customs of many Americans. For most of the Americans were Protestants, whose ideas were molded in large measure by the Hebrew Bible. Among Americans of all denominations Hebrew names like Abraham, Isaac, Benjamin, Aaron, Samuel, and Isaiah were quite popular. Their leading educators were Hebrew scholars; even the motto of Yale University was the Hebrew phrase, *y'hi or* (let there be light). When the Pilgrims completed their first harvest in 1621, they celebrated it with a thanksgiving festival patterned after the ancient Hebrew harvest festival, Sukkoth, which they knew about from their reading of the Old Testament.

Many of the speeches and writings of the leaders who protested against King George's tyrannical rule over the colonies were filled with quotations from the Hebrew Bible. The ministers in the churches compared King George to the wicked Pharaoh who oppressed the Hebrews, and they referred to George Washington as Moses. Preachers quoted from the Old Testament to prove that it was right to rebel against the king's harsh rule. When the colonies declared themselves independent from England, Thomas Jefferson, John Adams, and Benjamin Franklin were appointed to design an official seal for the new government. Their first suggestion was a scene depicting Moses leading the Hebrews to freedom across the Red Sea, with the Egyptians bogged down in the mud. The accompanying motto was to be, "Rebellion against tyrants is obedience to God."

It wasn't only through the example of their past history that Jews influenced the development of democratic ideas in the United States. Many Jews became ardent followers of Jefferson, who insisted that the purpose of government was to promote the common welfare, not the interests of the large property owners.

The Jeffersonians accused the Federalists, whose spokesman was Alexander Hamilton, of trying to establish in America the form of government that existed in Europe at that time—a monarchy in which the common people were treated as a lower class without any voice in the government. To fight this danger, many Jeffersonian clubs and newspapers sprang up in various parts of the country. Quite a number of Jews joined these clubs, and became officers in some of them. The Federalists called these clubs nests of radicals and revolutionaries, in order to scare people away from them. Some Federalists even emphasized the fact that a number of Jews were active in them, hoping that enough of the medieval sickness remained in the hearts of Americans to make them vote against anything with which Jews were connected.

When Benjamin Nones, a veteran of the Revolutionary War and vice-president of a Jeffersonian club, was attacked in a newspaper because he was a Jew, he wrote an answer and demanded that the newspaper print it. This occurred in August, 1800, a few months before the election by which Jefferson became the third President of the United States.

"I am a Jew," wrote Benjamin Nones. "Your reporter by

attempting to make me ridiculous, as a Jew, has made himself detestable, whatever religious persuasion may be dishonored by his adherence. But I am a Jew . . . and so were Abraham, and Isaac, and Moses and the Prophets, and so too were Christ and his apostles; and I feel no disgrace in ranking with such society. . . . I am a Jew, and if for no other reason, for that reason am I a Jeffersonian. . . . In the monarchies of Europe we are hunted from society . . . thrust out . . . objects of mockery and insult. . . . Among the nations of Europe we are inhabitants everywhere, but citizens nowhere. . . . In republics we have *rights*, in monarchies we live but to experience *wrongs*."

Like Nones, the Jews of America honored and respected their religion, and gloried in the history of the Jewish people. They were completely American in spirit, accepting wholeheartedly the idea of equality and democracy.

By the time of the Civil War the number of Jews in America had grown to about two hundred thousand, out of a total population of some thirty million. Only forty thousand of them lived in New York; the rest, in larger or smaller groups, had settled throughout New England, the South and the West.

Many Jews were active in the fight against slavery in the period of the 1840's and 1850's. Like other Americans, Jews attacked slavery as a denial of the sacred Declaration of Independence. Sometimes their opposition brought physical danger, as it did to August Bondi, Theodore Wiener, and Jacob Benjamin, three Jews who ran a trading post in Osawatomie, in the territory of Kansas.

The slave owners of the old South wanted to make sure that Kansas would come into the Union as a slave state. But the majority of the settlers in Kansas were opposed to slavery. The slave owners, therefore, sent agents into Kansas to terrorize the people into voting for slavery. One day a band of these hired hoodlums burned the store owned by Bondi, Wiener, and Benjamin, who were well-known enemies of slavery, and the three Jews were told to get out of Kansas. Along with other Kansans, they enlisted in the special army organized by John Brown, the famous abolitionist who was leading the fight against slavery in Kansas, and took part in a number of battles against the agents of the slave owners.

Americans of all faiths were working against slavery in various parts of the country, and a number of rabbis, particularly Dr. Bernard Felsenthal in Chicago, and Dr. David Einhorn in Baltimore, urged the Jews to join in the fight. And many Jews did.

There were some Jews, however, who defended slavery. Judah P. Benjamin, of Louisiana, was one of the pro-slavery leaders in the United States Senate. When the South seceded from the Union, Judah Benjamin was one of the organizers of the Confederacy. He served at one time or another as Attorney General, Secretary of War, and Secretary of State in the Cabinet of the Confederacy. Among other Jewish defenders of slavery was Rabbi Morris J. Raphall, of New York, who maintained that slavery was in keeping with God's wishes.

Among Christians there were differences over slavery, too. Ministers took sides with such passion that many churches in the South refused to have any relations with their sister churches in the North because of the attitude of northern ministers toward slavery. The Methodist churches of the South, for instance, organized themselves into the "Methodist Episcopal Church, South," and refused to meet with the northern branch of that faith. Southern Jews were also divided on the question of slavery, and quite a number of Southern Jews fought on the Union side.

All through the period of the building up of America, the Jews played a constructive role. From the start they were part of the hands and hearts and brains that made a nation out of the untamed wilderness the early settlers found on their arrival in the New World. They had no need to win special acceptance in those days, for they, like the settlers of other faiths, were farmers, merchants, and pioneers like their neighbors—immigrants all.

There were, of course, many people in the country who had prejudices; America was peopled by Europeans who quite naturally carried their prejudices with them to the New World. As succeeding waves of immigration washed over the land, the Old World prejudices kept cropping up, against Irish Catholics, against immigrants of this or that foreign country, against Jews. The earlier settlers had not regarded newcomers with a hostile eye—the land was big and broad, there was room for more. But as the country began to fill up in the early years of the twentieth century, voices were raised against the foreign-born, and some Americans developed an unfriendly attitude toward immigrants. Since Jews were entering the country in large numbers during this period, part of the anti-foreign agitation was directed against them.

Most of these Jews were from eastern Europe, as were large numbers of the non-Jewish immigrants in the 1880's and 1890's. The Jews had come from autocratic lands, where they had developed a distinct Jewish consciousness. Like other immigrants of that period, they clustered together in "ghetto-like" sections in New York and other large cities, by force of circumstances, not by law.

Unlike the native Jews who had grown up in America in the early years of its development, these immigrant Jews faced a period of adjustment to American ways. Their problem of adjustment was made more difficult by the fact that the frontiers of America were closing, and land was no longer available, as in the past, for the asking. They came in at a time when America faced many social and economic problems caused by the rapid industrialization of the country. Their adjustment was complicated further by the development of political anti-Semitism. This new type of organized, anti-Jewish activity must be taken into account for a proper understanding of the Jews in the modern world.

CHAPTER FOURTEEN

The Conspiracy Against Progress

THERE are people in many parts of the world who feel antagonistic toward Jews. They generally blame the Jews themselves for the existence of hostility against them, pointing out various hateful "Jewish" traits that caused the antagonism. But when the reasons they give to justify their dislike are examined, it becomes obvious that the "reasons" do not at all explain the cause of their anti-Semitism.

They accuse Jews, for instance, of being international bankers, but they see nothing wrong when Christians engage in the same business. If it is proved, furthermore, that only a handful of Jews are bankers on an international scale, and that most such bankers are Christians, the anti-Semite turns to another "reason." He dislikes Jews, then, because they are always trying to outdo everybody else. Any "reason" would do, because the hatred is in his heart; he simply looks for excuses to justify the unreasoning impulse to hate the Jew.

The anti-Semite would probably think you crazy if you told him that he was sick, that his hostility was a symptom of a dangerous disease within him. Yet he is sick, as sick inside as were the people of Toulouse who caused the death of Jean Calas, the Huguenot. It's an old sickness, this prejudice against Jews. Its seed was planted in the hostility of the early Church against the Jews; it flourished in the Middle Ages, when the Church deliberately sought to build a wall between Christian and Jew.

In the early days of Christianity, the close connection of Jesus with Jewish life and history was a source of confusion to the pagans who were then being converted to Christianity. These non-Jews knew very little about Jewish history or the events that led to the birth of the new religion. What confused them was the fact that the earliest Christians, the Judaeo-Christians, had called themselves Jews and had observed all the Jewish rituals and practices. The only difference, in those early days, was the acceptance by the Judaeo-Christians of Jesus as the Messiah. The New Testament had not yet been written; Christian religious doctrines were based upon interpretations of the Jewish holy books. These the Jews knew much better than the new converts. Since Jews and Christians mingled freely at that time, Christian leaders feared that the faith of the pagan converts might be weakened, particularly if they discussed their religious beliefs with Jews.

In those days, moreover, Judaism was a proselytizing religion, winning many adherents among the pagans in the Roman world. To the Christian missionaries, therefore, Judaism was a rival faith. Many propagandistic attacks on Judaism and the Jews were written in the heat of the religious rivalry of the time; some of these writings became part of the New Testament, the Christian Bible. Thus, children and adults, many of whom had never met a Jew personally, absorbed in the course of their religious education, which was based on the New Testament, a prejudice against Jews and Judaism.

Meanwhile, social and economic developments during the medieval period made the Jews appear to be different from the rest of the people of Europe. The feudal system forced the Jews off the manorial estates on which the vast majority of Europeans lived and worked, and the medieval guilds kept them out of the usual occupations and trades in the towns. They were thus forced out of the normal life of Europe altogether, and driven into such unpopular trades as moneylending and peddling of second-hand goods.

Even though Christians in the Middle Ages never met a Jew, to them he was a strange species. He was the "Devil," accused of every "devilish" event, such as plagues or bad harvests. And when they did meet a Jew, he seemed strange because of his different mode of life and work. The Jew became a type, not an individual. All Jews were alike, so far as the popular conception of them was concerned. Any discreditable thing held to be true of a single Jew was easily, therefore, believed to be true of all Jews. Accusations against them did not require proof because an unfriendly attitude toward Jews was continually being implanted in the minds of Europeans in medieval times.

Even the literature portrayed Jews in a hostile light. Great writers like Chaucer, Shakespeare, and Marlowe, when they dealt with Jewish characters, gave a distorted picture of them, in spite of the fact that they had probably never seen a Jew at close hand; for the Jews had been banished from England in 1290, years before these writers were born, and were not readmitted until the 1650's, years after they had died.

Thus, the very culture pattern of Christian Europe included an unflattering picture of the Jew. Centuries of continuous anti-Jewish teaching made the prejudice so much a part of the Christian attitude that it seemed to be in the air people breathed. The very word "Jew" called forth distasteful images and associations. The Jews could live like veritable angels and it would matter little—the anti-Jewish germ was ever-present, infecting each new generation.

This anti-Jewish feeling became a handy weapon for unscrupulous people. A lord in debt to a Jewish moneylender could liquidate his debt by getting rid of the moneylender altogether. All that was necessary was to get the serfs or townspeople worked up to an angry mood about the Jews; an attack on the Jewish community would follow, and both the Jewish banker and the record of the debt would disappear, coincidentally. Christian merchants could, in the same way, rid themselves of Jewish competitors by getting them expelled from their towns and cities.

People like these helped keep alive the animosity toward Jews and Judaism by manufacturing out of thin air accusations that aroused people against the Jews—that they had poisoned the wells, that they had desecrated the HOLY WAFERS in the church, that they had killed a Christian child so they could use its blood for ritual purposes during the Passover celebration. In time, these became part of the legends and libels that one generation handed on to the next. Some of these unfriendly stories are still current in our own day—for instance, one of *The Canterbury Tales* by Geoffrey Chaucer deals with an incident in twelfth-century England in which the Jews were accused of the ritual murder of a Christian boy, St. Hugh of Lincoln. Such stories, which became part of European culture, simply reinforced the prejudice that people in each generation had picked up in early childhood, and continued it.

But certain events and developments in European life seemed to give promise that anti-Jewish prejudices would become weaker, even disappear. The Protestant Reformation served to drain off some of the animosity that had been directed against the Jews when they were the only people in Europe of a different religion. With the rise of various Protestant faiths, the Jews were no longer the only ones who were "unlike" in that respect.

And when the ghetto walls were broken down and Jews were permitted to enter occupations hitherto open to Christians only, Jews became more and more like their neighbors in practically all matters except their religion. The growing importance of trade and manufacturing, furthermore, gave a new respectability to the work Jews had once been forced into: "moneylending" became banking, and "peddling" became merchandizing, two very important functions in the world of trade and commerce. They were no longer "Jewish" occupations, for large numbers of Christians had now entered them.

Again, in feudal times Jews had been regarded as outsiders. Only those people "belonged" who were part of the manor or town; and for that one had to be a Christian. But when national states were formed, the idea began to germinate that a person was part of the country simply because he lived somewhere in it. In western Europe the Jews began to be accepted as citizens like their neighbors. They "belonged" too.

Meanwhile, the relation between religion and government was undergoing a change. In the medieval period, the purpose of government as well as of life was to insure "Christian" living—the State was looked upon as merely an agency of the Church in its task of bringing "salvation" to people. But in the business-minded nineteenth century, the merchants and manufacturers turned the government into an agency to insure them opportunities for business and profits. In the minds of people, the Church and the State were beginning to be regarded as separate and distinct entities, each with its own special functions.

Furthermore, by the nineteenth century, people's attitudes toward religion itself had changed. Up to the Protestant Reformation, the Roman Catholic faith had been regarded quite generally as the only true road to salvation. In most European countries, the rulers recognized the Roman Church as the official religion of their domains. But when a large part of Europe turned Protestant, many people objected to this recognition, since it placed one faith above all others. A demand arose for the separation of Church and State altogether. With no official religion for the State, all religions would be placed on an equal basis, and all religious groups would have the same rights and privileges. Before the separation of Church and State, governments had often discriminated against adherents of the unofficial religions.

This movement for the separation of Church and State, based on the principle of religious equality, helped the Jews as well as the Protestants. For Judaism had been attacked for years as a contemptible, Satanic invention. The democratic idea of equality, of religions as well as of people, compelled the recognition of Judaism's proper place as one of the world's great faiths.

One of the most important reasons why people were ready to accept other religions as valid—something the medieval mind simply could not do, as the holy wars and the attacks on heresy prove—was that a scientific revolution was in progress during the nineteenth century. Man's ideas, traditions, and beliefs, as well as the phenomena of nature, were searchingly examined, as though under a microscope. Sir Charles Lyell's *Principles of Geology* showed that the earth had developed its form through natural processes over hundreds of thousands of years. Not the divine command, but changes in temperature, and floods, rains and snows, over aeons of time had produced the layers of the earth's crust and the minerals in it, said the geologists. Charles Darwin's *Origin of Species* showed that life itself had evolved slowly over millions of years, some species becoming extinct, while new species were being developed in the process of evolution.

These and other disclosures of science as to the nature of the universe caused people to question the doctrine of orthodox religion, that God had created the world as it is, in six days. Perhaps religions also were the product of evolution! From this doubt concerning the scientific accuracy of the Bible, people went on to challenge the truth of certain statements in the Bible and the religious dogmas based on them. The scientific trend thus became a grave problem to the religious leaders. The danger was no longer the mere existence of other, and rival, faiths; Christian leaders were worried about the weakening of faith altogether. This also weakened the traditional argument that Judaism was a danger to pure Christian faith.

In the nineteenth century, therefore, the religious prejudice against the Jews lost some of the hostile sting that had been inherited from medieval times, especially since the Jews had begun to assume a more normal role in European life. In many countries of western Europe, in fact, they were made to feel quite welcome.

Oddly enough, this new situation created new problems for the Jews. The scientific revolution weakened the authority of the Bible in Judaism too; like the Christians, many Jews began to question the beliefs and practices that had developed in Jewish life from Biblical times on.

The social and economic changes in the position of the Jews also affected their outlook. When they had lived in the ghettos, their lives had been regulated by the Talmud and the ghetto councils; every activity had been guided according to the religious laws of Judaism. But now that they lived and worked in predominantly Christian communities, they found it difficult to continue many of the practices that had become accepted as essential for Jewish living. Jewish storekeepers in Christian neighborhoods, for instance, found it necessary to do business on Saturdays—a day on which Jews had scrupulously refrained from labor heretofore.

Other religious customs of the ghetto were disregarded by many Jews, particularly those who were now moving in the same circles as their Christian friends. The strict dietary laws, for example, prevented their eating in Christian homes with an easy conscience; food for Jews had to be selected and prepared according to Talmudic regulations; and if their friends decided to have a snack in a restaurant, and only non-Kosher restaurants were available, the Jews either had to disregard the Jewish law or break up the party.

Some Jews began to question whether the Talmudic rules had to be observed to the last detail, if such observance meant that a Jew had to separate himself from his Christian neighbors. This had not been a serious problem in the ghetto days; the walls had acted as a barrier against intimate association with Christians, and the completely Jewish atmosphere inside the walls made the Talmudic rules part of the social pattern. The emancipation made some of the ghetto customs seem like foreign folkways to European-minded Jews, and the scientific revolution weakened the authority of the Bible and the Talmud on which many of the laws and customs had been based. Some Jews actually turned away from religious observance altogether, for the same reasons that made many Christians turn away from their own faiths.

While most Jews remained loyal to the faith of their fathers, many did feel uneasy about a number of practices of the religion. For some, the services in the synagogues, held entirely in Hebrew, became meaningless, since they did not know the language well. Some Jews also became critical of the wearing of hats during the services. In the Middle East, where Judaism originated, the covering of the head was a way of showing respect for people as well as for the Lord. But in the European world where such respect was shown by removing one's hat—in public buildings, in people's homes, and when one met friends on the street—

it seemed out of place. There were also Jews who were disturbed by the traditional custom of seating women in special sections of the synagogue, apart from the men, during services; it didn't seem to fit in with the democratic movement for equality between the sexes.

There was also concern about some of the prayers of the traditional liturgy. There were a number of traditional prayers which besought God to hasten the time when all Jews would be reunited in Zion. This seemed to imply that the Jews were an exiled nation, and that those who lived outside of Palestine were homeless, wandering strangers. But the Jews of the Western world were beginning to feel completely at home in the countries of their birth. To them, their native land was their homeland. They were citizens, part of the national family, and wholeheartedly loyal to their native countries; they did not want to live anywhere else.

Many religious leaders and scholars among the Europeanized Jews began to feel it necessary to bring the meaning and practice of Judaism up to date. One of these, Leopold Zunz, convinced many Jews that there was nothing irreligious in making changes in their traditional beliefs and practices. He showed that Jewish religious rules had undergone many changes in the past, whenever Jews had come into contact with new ideas and customs. Other religious leaders, among them laymen like Israel Jacobson, and rabbis like Abraham Geiger, also urged that Judaism be brought into harmony with the new knowledge and the new conditions of the times.

Under their influence many changes were made in the manner of observing the religion. The prayers were translated into the languages spoken in the countries the Jews lived in; rabbis began to preach sermons in those tongues; organ music and mixed choirs were introduced to make the services more beautiful and impressive; men and women were seated together, and no hats were worn in some of the synagogues. Many of the traditional prayers were left out, particularly those dealing with the hope that the Jews would one day again make sacrifices at the restored Temple in Jerusalem. New prayers were written emphasizing the ethical purpose of the religion, rather than the rituals and ceremonials. The leaders of Reform Judaism, as this movement in Jewish life came to be known, stressed the ideals of the Prophets of Israel, rather than the Talmudic regulations and the ghetto-developed customs.

Many rabbis protested against all these reforms. They felt that the Jewish religion had been given the people by God; and to them, any tampering with the traditional methods of observing it meant the abandonment of the faith altogether. These Orthodox rabbis insisted that there was but one way to observe Judaism, and that was the way the Bible and the Talmud directed—in other words, in the way the Jews of the ghettos had observed it. Other rabbis, known as Conservative, took a middle position. There was room for some modernizing of Judaism, they said, but they also revered the traditional practices of the Jewish people and were loath to change them.

In the Christian world, as in the Jewish world, the medieval emphasis upon religious conformity began to disappear, particularly in those countries where religion was removed from state politics through the separation of Church and State. Religion became a personal matter, to be decided by one's own conscience, not something to be enforced by government decree. Jews were therefore no longer singled out for attack just because their religious beliefs and practices were different.

People's views concerning the purpose of government also underwent a change in the nineteenth century. Large numbers accepted the democratic idea that the chief aim of government was to guarantee the welfare of the individual, no matter what religion or creed he adhered to. In the spirit of the time, many of the landless peasants began to demand that the big estates be divided to make more land available for the common people. The workers, too, looked to the government for help in getting better wages and working conditions. Political parties like the Socialists even suggested that the government take over various industries and operate them, not for profit, but for the benefit of all the people.

Many people saw great hope in the nineteenth century; the great achievements in industry and in man's understanding of life and the universe made them feel that people would learn, in time, to live side by side in harmony, accepting one another as equals, respecting one another's beliefs and customs.

But not everybody was ready to accept the changes that nineteenth century developments were causing. Certain groups actually disliked the temper of the times; for them the "well-ordered world" of the Middle Ages held greater appeal. The big landowners had lost many of the privileges and powers they had enjoyed in bygone days, and they feared the growing demand for the division of their estates. The big industrialists and businessmen were disturbed by the growth of labor unions and the growing demand for government ownership of public utilities and other industries.

Some Church leaders were also not enthusiastic over the liberal movements of the nineteenth century. The Church in the past had controlled the education of people and had been able to concentrate attention on the doctrines of the faith. But now, public school systems were being established by governments, schools in which the teaching of sectarian religious doctrines was prohibited. The state schools were even permitting the teaching of the Darwinian theory of evolution and other scientific material that brought into question age-old religious beliefs. Besides, Church officials were becoming worried about the demands some people were making that Church property be taxed like all other property.

There appeared to be no hope for these groups who thirsted to revive the autocratic system of the past, so strong did the liberal spirit seem. But there was a movement afoot in Europe which these groups were able finally to fashion into a powerful weapon with which to attack nineteenth century progress.

This movement, nationalism, started out as an innocent enough feeling of pride in one's country, a glorification of the culture and accomplishments of one's nation. But the nationalist literature of the latter half of the nineteenth century harped on the idea that the people of a nation had certain "blood ties." The German nationalists developed the theme that the Germans were a "race"—and a superior one, at that; and that the German "national bloodstream" possessed nobler tastes, ways of thinking and morals than other races. To the German nationalists, these were "German" qualities that came to the people through their "blood" and stamped them as a "master race." And just as the Germans had a noble national character, they said, so were there other peoples who had ignoble and unworthy national characteristics.

In nationalist jargon there were two races, the "Aryan" and the "Semite." The fact that these terms referred originally not to races, but to certain languages spoken in various parts of the world, did not bother the nationalists; they were not interested in scientific truth. Since the "Aryan" and "Semitic" languages were so different, they said, the peoples who spoke them must be radically different, too. The nationalists proceeded to use these handy terms to label certain "racial cultures"—"Aryan" meaning the noble peoples who had contributed all that was good in Western civilization; the "Semitic," a "cultural bloodstream" full of poisonous qualities. Since Hebrew was a Semitic language, the Jews became "Semites" in the literature of the nationalists, and all the bad things they attributed to "Semitic blood" became identified with the Jews.

The German historian, von Treitschke, called the Jews Germany's misfortune, "Semites" whose base culture was poisoning the golden-pure German "bloodstream." Eugen Dühring, another German nationalist, characterized the Jews as destroyers, not creators. And Max Stirner, another nationalist, claimed that the Jews had never progressed beyond the primitive stage of civilization; they must therefore not be permitted to take an active part in German life, else they would debase the "master race's" culture.

Nothing was sacred to these nationalist "anti-Semites,"

least of all the truth. Bent on showing that nothing good could come from the Jews, some of them attacked Christianity too, since that faith had originated out of Judaism. Nietzsche, the German philosopher, dismissed the ethical teachings of Judaism and Christianity as unworthy of Germans; they added up to a "slave morality" that was not fit for the "master race" of conquering "Aryans." But other racists, like Houston Stewart Chamberlain, classified Christianity as "Aryan" in spirit, and depicted the Jews as enemies of both Germanism and Christianity.

Ordinarily, much of this theory would have had little effect upon people, since there was little of logic, science, or truth in it. But it was about Jews, a people against whom a great prejudice had existed from medieval times. If the prejudice had depended solely upon religious differences, it might have worn off in time because of the changed attitude toward religion. But "anti-Semitism" was made part of the exciting feeling of nationalism, which was capturing the imagination of so many Europeans. It gave the medieval germ a new lease on life, only now it had a different refrain: the Jews were accused of being an alien people who could not be assimilated into the national family. In Germany, a Protestant country, Adolf Stöcker, the chaplain at the court of Kaiser Wilhelm I, was able to organize a political party solely on the basis of anti-Semitism. In Vienna, the Catholics organized a similar party.

All of this anti-Semitic propaganda and activity was made to order for those who represented the upper, privileged classes. Bismarck, the chancellor of Germany, used the rising anti-Semitism as a means of gaining control of the government for antidemocratic purposes. The German

Liberal party, with its large following, had been standing in his way; it opposed his militarization of the country and also insisted on various democratic reforms in the government. There were a number of Jews in the Liberal party. Bismarck spread the fiction that the party was a Jewish movement, and his agitators kept hammering away at the fact that Jews were members of it.

All the newspapers that attacked Bismarck were also called Jewish. Everyone who opposed his policies was called a Jew or a tool of the Jews. Every effort was made to convince people that Bismarck's party and policies were German, while the opposition came only from the Jews, or Christians who had "sold out" to the Jews. And since the anti-Semitic leaders had made many people believe that there really was a "Jewish conspiracy," many people fell into Bismarck's net; they turned away from the Liberal party. When the Liberal party was weakened, and Bismarck gained firmer control of the government, he embarked on a more extensive militarization of the country, as well as on a program of greater aid to industrialists and landowners.

Of course, not everybody was fooled. Many Protestants and Catholics denounced the lies of the anti-Semites. But that did not stop the agitation, for the ruling classes had found a wonderful weapon for weakening the democratic front; simply by arousing the people over a false issue, they could divide them. Almost any spellbinder, anyone who could excite people, or who could put a few anti-Semitic sentences together in a readable form, could find financial support and even protection from the powerful groups who profited from their propaganda.

The prejudices of old, plus the newly-created ones, made the cultural climate of Europe once again hostile to Jews. Agitators organized boycotts against Jewish stores and firms. They provoked Jews to anger so that fights and brawls could be started. Jews found themselves unwelcome in various schools, clubs, hotels, and resorts.

Even in France, the country that gave Europe its ideals of equality and brotherhood, an anti-Semitic movement came into being. By 1891 it was strong enough to elect a number of deputies in the French legislature who publicly urged that the Jews be expelled from the country. Then in 1894, came the famous Dreyfus case.

In that year, a French army officer discovered that certain military plans and secrets had been sold to Germany. The culprit was Count Esterhazy, a French officer and a member of the aristocracy. But it simply would not do to have an aristocrat brought to public disgrace. So a friend of Esterhazy, Lieutenant-Colonel Henry, secretly had some documents forged in order to throw suspicion upon another officer, Captain Alfred Dreyfus. Dreyfus was brought to trial and quickly convicted; he was dishonorably discharged, and condemned to Devil's Island.

This was a brilliant move, for Alfred Dreyfus was a Jew, the first Jew to have become a member of the General Staff of the French Army. It was a "natural" for the French anti-Semites, and they came out in full pack, calling all Jews traitors and aliens who couldn't be trusted. The monarchists blamed the Republic for harboring treason in the army—it could only have happened, they said, because democracy and equality had been carried too far. The aristocrats joined the monarchists since they had always fared better when kings, not commoners, ruled. For the Church, a change in the government was also an event to be hoped for, one that held the promise of more power for it in the government, and particularly over the educational system.

With support coming from these groups, a strong movement was organized against the Jews and the democratic government of France. It became almost dangerous to voice liberal ideas, so effectively did the anti-Semites connect democracy with the "treasonous" Jews. Attacks were also made upon the Protestant minority of France, particularly after a Protestant member of the French Senate declared that he doubted Dreyfus' guilt.

There were many who suspected dirty work, among them, Colonel Picquart, Georges Clemenceau, and Emile Zola, but their protesting voices were drowned out by the hysteria that had been whipped up. When Zola published his famous "J'Accuse" letter, courageously accusing the monarchists and the clerical party of plotting to destroy French democracy through their campaign against the Jews, he was prosecuted for slander and banished from the country.

The anti-Semites kept the temperature of the country at fever level; Frenchmen became divided into Dreyfusards and anti-Dreyfusards, and at election time voted accordingly. The air was so laden with prejudice that a great many monarchists and anti-Semites were elected to the government. Attacks against Jews broke out in various parts of France. And in the midst of all the turmoil an attempt was made by some of the reactionary leaders to destroy the Republic and put a king on the throne. Thus

was anti-Semitism deliberately used as a political device
to divert the attention of the majority of the population
from the real aims of those who opposed democracy.

For ten years the hate campaign went on, but Zola,
Picquart, Clemenceau, and others gradually rallied the
French people to the side of truth and common sense.
Colonel Henry's forgeries were exposed for what they
were. He committed suicide; Count Esterhazy fled to England; and Dreyfus was exonerated and restored to his rank
in the army. The Republic survived; it even became
strengthened as the anti-Semites lost favor.

There were other times when the anti-Semites received
setbacks, but they continued their propaganda. And when
hard times, unemployment, or other crises hit some country—when the people began to make demands upon their
governments for help—at such times funds for the anti-
Semites increased, as did the scale of their activities. Nor
was it only the Jews who were used as a wedge between
people, to separate and confuse them by inflaming one
group against another. The Irish Catholics were labeled
as the "menace" in Protestant America in the 1850's and
the 1880's, while in Moslem Turkey, it was the Christian
Armenians, and in Hindu India the Moslems. In the southern states of America, the Negro served as a handy scape-
goat, and on the West Coast the Chinese and Japanese.

Anti-Semitism is as widespread as it is in the Western
World because in all Christian lands the prejudice against
Jews has been passed on from generation to generation—
in some, through the type of religious training certain Christian churches give; and in others, through the attitudes of
parents and the general community, as they have been con-

ditioned by literature, stories, and legends. And the prejudice has been kept deliberately alive by the propaganda of anti-Semitic groups with political aims.

The anti-Jewish culture pattern was a grave danger to the existence of the Jews, but they were not the only ones who were harmed by it. A great many Christians were victimized as a result of their own anti-Semitism. Adolph Hitler, financed by wealthy industrialists and corporations seeking their own ends, organized the anti-Jewish prejudices of Germany into a mighty political weapon. Through anti-Semitism, he created great anxiety and unrest among the German people at a time when there was widespread unemployment and insecurity in the country. Some actually believed, as Hitler told them, that the Jews were the cause of all the misery in the country. Some Germans hoped Hitler's party would win so that they could lay their hands on the business and property of the Jews. Others imagined there would be jobs for them when the Jews were driven out of German life. Some were simply criminally minded and saw in Hitler's movement a chance for plunder and violence.

When Hitler came to power, many got what they were hoping for. But the German people as a whole also lost a great deal. They lost their freedom to speak and act; they lost their right to organize themselves into political parties of their own choice; and they lost the right to organize unions to gain economic security.

Anti-Semitism and race hatred became part of the creed and philosophy of the Nazi state; it was taught in the schools, in the clubs, wherever Germans gathered together. It became a definite part of a German's outlook on life. All the Nazis needed, to keep the people in line, was to whip up hysteria against the Jews; the Germans became like robots as a result of the Nazi propaganda, ready to do the bidding of their Fuehrer no matter how revolting the task assigned them. Years of anti-Semitic teaching had made them a people bereft of moral sensibility; centuries of Christian training had been erased from their hearts by the few years of Nazi attack upon all religious virtues as "Jewish."

Under the Nazis, anti-Semitism became a flourishing international movement. They financed anti-Semitic outfits everywhere, prepared material for them, and assisted them in every way possible. Through anti-Semitism, they had deprived the Germans of sanity; through it they hoped to divide and weaken whatever country the Nazis planned to attack. In this way the virus was spread; it reached lands where it had never become part of the culture pattern of the people—in Arab lands, for instance, where Jews had lived for centuries on amicable terms with their neighbors.

Organized anti-Semitism brought great suffering to the Jews, especially during the Hitlerian period when six million Jews were killed in Germany and in the countries which the Nazis had overrun. Besides the loss of life, untold property was confiscated, and the cultural institutions the European Jews had developed over the centuries were destroyed. But the rest of the world had suffered too.

Many Christians years ago realized the danger that anti-Semitism represented. Many organizations came into being to fight this immoral movement. Much effective work is being done to bring the disease under control. It is being fought through the churches, through books, magazines, and movies, in cultural organizations, in unions; on many fronts, racial and religious prejudice is being attacked, in the hope that brotherhood and equality may some day overcome the feeling of prejudice.

It was only natural that the anti-Semitic movement of the nineteenth century should have profound effects upon Jewish life and thought. Many Jews began to feel a definite sense of insecurity. Their attitudes and ideas began to be influenced by the wall of distrust and hatred that was being erected against them. Just as they had had to adjust themselves to the free air of Europe after their emancipation from the ghetto, Jews now had to adjust themselves to the unfriendly attitudes the modern anti-Semites had developed against them among their neighbors. How they adjusted themselves depended in large measure upon the kind of political, social, and economic system under which they lived. The picture of the Jews in the contemporary world, therefore, reflects the variations in their outlook and activity caused by these different systems.

CHAPTER FIFTEEN

The Jews in Three Worlds

THERE are Jews in many countries of the world, but the three major Jewish communities of 1949, in point of population, are in the United States (about five million); the Soviet Union (more than two million); and the state of Israel (about 800,000). In these and the other countries they have been influenced in one way or another by the development of nationalism and anti-Semitism.

Even though some of the problems the Jews faced, in whatever lands they lived, were similar, Jewish life did not develop according to the same pattern everywhere. The attitude toward Jewish traditions, religion, and culture that Jews developed differed from one country to another. Nevertheless, the story of Jewish life in the three major communities can give a good insight into the trends in Jewish life today.

The Dreyfus affair was a shocking experience to the Jews of the world, particularly painful for those Jews of western Europe who had completely integrated themselves into the life and culture of their native lands. Many had completely dissociated themselves from the Jewish religion, although they did not embrace any other faith. And some who still identified themselves as members of the Jewish faith, nevertheless took very little part in the affairs of the Jewish community beyond contributing their communal dues and gifts to Jewish charities. Many western Jews deliberately turned away from Jewish customs and folkways that had come out of ghetto life, regarding them as "foreign." They had become ardent nationalists; the culture they valued was the culture of the nation of which they and their non-Jewish neighbors were a part.

But the anti-Semitic outbreak in France, and the ultranationalist agitation in their own countries, left them dazed. The civilization the Europeanized Jews had come to prize no longer gave them satisfaction. It was only a thin veneer, a shiny surface. Underneath it, just barely covered, was anti-Jewish prejudice, the ugly heritage of the Middle Ages. To their neighbors they were not really fellow Frenchmen or Germans or Austrians—they were just Jews, to be accepted under sufferance, if at all.

Although they had little contact with Jewish life and culture, they were being identified in the popular mind as Jews: as members of a people who were attacked as outsiders, alien to the national family. For years they had believed themselves to be completely accepted members of the national family; now they felt they were being cast out. A feeling of homelessness seized many Jews.

This, said Theodor Herzl, a Viennese newspaper correspondent who was living in Paris when the Dreyfus case broke, was the greatest tragedy of the Jews: they had no state of their own to give them political protection and the feeling of belonging. He called upon his fellow Jews the world over to band together and establish such a state—a Jewish national home, where freedom and equality would be guaranteed. Then would the Jew be on a par with the nationals of other countries.

His call stirred to action a great many Jews who for years had been feeling uneasy about their position in Europe. In Russia and eastern Europe generally, Jews were continually under attack, the government officials themselves frequently organizing the anti-Semitic pogroms. In eastern Europe the Jews had developed a feeling of peoplehood, like the national minorities among whom they lived, only they did not live on soil they could claim as their own by virtue of having lived on it for centuries under their own rulers, as could the Poles, for example. To many Jews of eastern Europe, therefore, the idea of a Jewish national homeland held great appeal.

In western Europe, too, many Jews responded, especially those who felt they were not really being accepted as equal citizens, even though they still had the right to vote. It was difficult for them to conceive of themselves as a people as did the East-European Jews, since they did not regard their Jewishness as constituting a national culture. To them it was no more than a religious identification, or a sentimental attachment to traditional customs inherited from parents and grandparents. But now, disturbed by active anti-Semitism, many of them began to seek a closer identification with the persecuted Jews of other lands whose sense of homelessness was more acute.

Some Jews began to feel that what they had done, and were doing, to help build up the countries they lived in, was wasted, in a sense, since the Jews in those countries were being regarded by many as outsiders. They longed to put their energies to work on something they could feel as their very own. The vision of building a Jewish homeland, a nation of their own, was a powerful drive that brought many rootless Jews to the Zionist movement that Herzl had inspired.

A very large number of Jews all over the world, however, did not accept Herzl's ideas. They did not wish to leave the countries in which their families had lived for generations. They knew that Palestine could not possibly absorb the more than fifteen million Jews that existed in the world at that time. Most of them did not oppose the efforts of Jews to build up the land of Palestine; they gave it financial support, so that it could be made into a haven for the more hard-pressed Jews of Europe. They did, however, deny the Zionist claim that the establishment of a Jewish state would solve the problem of anti-Semitism for Jews who would be living outside the Jewish state, assuming that it could be established.

Many such Jews had not given way to despair at the apparently crawling pace with which the democratic movement approached its goal of brotherhood and equality. In time, they believed, through education and through working together, people would learn to live together on equal terms. They preferred to fight anti-Semitism in their native lands, to improve social and economic conditions in their own countries to such an extent that people would have no need to hate and fear.

The creation of a Jewish state in Palestine was never, actually, the unanimous expression of the Jewish people; but Zionism became, in time, a movement of great proportions and great fervor. It attracted tens of thousands to whom a Jewish Palestine spelled security, a sense of belonging, an end of homelessness. It attracted people to whom working for Zion gave a sense of satisfaction; it gave Jews who had dissociated themselves from the Jewish religion a sense of identification with the Jewish people. For Palestine had always been looked upon by Jews as inseparable from Jewish history, lore, and tradition. It was the scene of past glory; it became to them now a symbol of the continuity of the Jewish tradition, and a guarantee of the rebirth of Jewish culture.

In 1896, when Herzl gave the movement its impetus, Palestine was ruled by the Turks. A few thousand Jews lived in the barren and run-down country, and its poor economic conditions did not lure Jews in large numbers. Before it could be made into a habitable country a great deal of pioneering work would have to be done. But the sultan of Turkey stood in the way, refusing to ease the restrictions against Jews; he also refused to give the Zionists any guarantee of political security.

Not until 1917 were the Jews able to begin the great work of preparing Palestine for future statehood. In that year, Arthur James Balfour, on behalf of the British government, made a declaration of sympathy with the aspirations of the Zionists. He promised the aid of his government in the project of building a national home in Palestine for the Jewish people. The British were at war at the time with Germany and Turkey; the Balfour Declaration, they reasoned, would gain them the support of the Jews of the world in the trying days of the First World War, since Turkey would have to be defeated before the declaration could go into effect.

The Zionist movement, which had been growing steadily, particularly in eastern Europe, now began to win greater support in every Jewish community the world over. Even Jews who did not favor the Zionist demand for a Jewish-dominated state in Palestine contributed large amounts of money for the economic development of the country, in the hope that it could be developed into a refuge for thousands of Jews who were made homeless by the events of the First World War.

Training camps were established in many parts of the world to prepare Jews for work and life in Palestine. With money contributed to a special fund by Jews the world over, acres upon acres of land were bought in Palestine, to be owned by the Jewish community there. Orange groves, farms, and factories were established, irrigation systems were built, and thousands of Jews from many lands, but especially from eastern Europe, came to Palestine to transform it into a modern country. They made desert wastes bloom and flower. They built cities and villages, they poured their hearts into their work, and Palestine began to thrive.

The ancient festivals of the Jews, which had originated in Palestine, they were able once again to celebrate on historic soil. The events of Jewish history, from ancient times on, were taught in the schools with as much emphasis as America, for instance, gives to its history in American schools. The Patriarchs, the Prophets, the ancient kings and generals, the rabbis of old—all the experiences of the Jewish past became part of the curriculum of the Palestinian Jewish schools. Jewish culture became the main loyalty and consideration of the Jews of Palestine.

The Hebrew language, somewhat modernized, became once again their living tongue, used at home, in the streets, at work, and in the schools, colleges, and universities. Once again, Hebrew began to express the hopes and joys, the defeats and successes of a people with a common bond, a people whose future was bound up with a land they could look upon as their very own. And out of Palestine flowed not only the products of farm and factory, but also the products of the spirit: books, songs, dances, plays, and folk stories that grew out of the revived national life of the Jews.

One of the exciting developments within Palestine was the creation of many co-operative farm communities, *kibbutzim* built from the ground up by Jewish labor. Despite dangers, hardships, and heartbreaks, the Jewish pioneers built hundreds of such colonies; it was hard to discourage them, for they were building in the name of their people. They were producing and building, they were developing their land, *Eretz Yisroel*, the "Land of Israel."

On the co-operatives they worked not for individual gain and betterment but for the welfare of the whole community. It made it more meaningful to them to work that way, knowing that in the very land where they themselves were living, the ancient Hebrew Prophets had preached just that kind of life—co-operation and consideration—to the end that all the inhabitants would enjoy the good things the land had to offer.

Unfortunately, however, they were not living on an island off by themselves. Their land was situated on the Mediterranean, close to the rich oil fields of Iran, Iraq, and Arabia, to the east; and the Suez Canal to the southwest. Pipelines from these oil fields passed through Palestine to Mediterranean ports; and the Suez Canal was one of the important life lines of British Empire trade. Arab rulers owned the oil, which British companies wanted to exploit, and Arab peoples lived near the Canal. The British government, therefore, sought in every way possible to maintain the good will and friendship of the Arab rulers. Because of this, Britain's attitude toward the Jews of Palestine gradually grew hostile, for the Arab ruling classes wanted Palestine to be an Arab state, not a Jewish one. To please the Arab rulers, the British government began to restrict Jewish immigration to Palestine, and also limited the amount of land Jews could buy.

The result of this policy was to dam the flow of Jews toward Palestine. The horror of it was that these restrictions were enforced at a time when Hitler's murderous policy toward the Jews was at its height. Thousands might have been saved from death in the crematories and the concentration camps if the European Jews could have entered Palestine.

The total Jewish population of Palestine at the time of the Second World War was about six hundred thousand, while the Arab population was over a million. This situation made the Zionist demand for a Jewish state seem undemocratic, since the Jews were a definite minority in Palestine. The Arabs not only were in the majority, but they, too, had historic claims to Palestine. They, too, had developed a national feeling; and just as Jews in other parts of the world worked for a Jewish state in Palestine so did Arabs outside of Palestine organize to make the country an Arab state.

Britain, to keep its control over Palestine, played one national feeling against the other. It occasionally passed decrees or issued statements raising the hopes of the Jews that they would win out in the future. Palestinian Jewish groups were thus induced to back Britain as a true friend of the Jews. Then she turned around and enforced restrictions against the Jews to show the Arabs that Britain really supported the Arab claims. With Britain keeping the country in a state of division and turmoil, a spirit of hostility arose between Arabs and Jews, even though Jews and Moslems had for centuries lived together in peace. Their bickering and occasional fighting made it seem necessary for the British to retain control over Palestine as the only power able to keep order in the country.

World opinion was finally aroused to such a point that the United Nations took a hand in the situation, for the turmoil in the Holy Land made people fear a possible outbreak of war. The General Assembly of the United Nations, therefore, on November 29, 1947, decided to terminate Britain's mandate over Palestine, and to partition the country into two states, one Arab and the other Jewish. It allowed for a transition period during which both peoples were to organize independent democratic governments, which were to co-operate on certain economic matters necessary for the well-being of both countries.

Immediately after the United Nations decision, the Arab rulers of Egypt, Saudi Arabia, Iraq, Syria, Lebanon, Ye-men, and Trans-Jordan, bound together as a league of Arab states, began to make war against the Jews of Palestine, to keep them from setting up a state. There was sporadic fighting all through the five and a half months that Britain was to keep its mandate over Palestine. The fighting cost more than a thousand Jewish and Arab lives, but the United Nations did nothing to enforce the partition plan or to stop the Arab attacks.

While the Arab countries were able to buy planes, arms, and ammunition, the Jews of Palestine had no legal agency to get such supplies for their own defense, since they had no legally recognized government as yet. The Jews, moreover, were not able, legally, to bring many Jews into the country during the transition period; the army and navy of Britain kept illegal immigration down to a comparatively small number. But the Arab states were able to send between three and seven thousand armed and equipped troops into Palestine with seeming ease.

Nevertheless, *Haganah*, the well-organized Jewish army, more than held its own. Many of its members had seen service in the Second World War on the side of the victorious Allies in Africa and Europe. Haganah, moreover, was not only defending its own land, but it was fighting to keep the land open for the scores of thousands of homeless Jews in D.P. (Displaced Persons) camps of Europe. And when the transition period came to an end, the Jews of Palestine, on May 14, 1948, hoisted high the *Mogen David* (Star of David) and proclaimed their independence as the state of Israel.

They were now a nation in their own land, with their own language, and with institutions and folkways uniquely their own—the products of the life the Jews of Palestine and of other countries had established there through the years of settlement. As such, they had lived in a world quite different from Jewish communities elsewhere. In their world Jewish culture was national, a distinctive culture produced out of the living experience of the Jews who had built up the country.

While no other Jewish community is like the Israelis, as the Jewish citizens of Israel are called, insofar as cultural and political organization is concerned, they are not the only Jews who think of themselves as a national group. In the Soviet Union, Jews are also organized as a national group, and the Soviet government actually recognizes them as such.

Under the czars the Jews of Russia had developed a national consciousness. Their culture was based in large part on their life together in the Pale of Settlement; they had governed themselves in the communities of the Pale in the spirit of the Talmudic laws, and out of their experiences over the centuries had come definitely Jewish folk customs and a literature in their mother tongue, Yiddish.

There were other national minorities in Russia, but unlike them the Jews had not dwelt in a well-defined territory within the empire that had been their own, historic national home. While other national groups, like the Poles, dreamed of freedom from czarist rule so they could govern themselves in their own land, most Russian Jews hoped for the establishment of a Jewish homeland in Palestine. Then they could escape the pogroms and insecurity of their position in Russia, and at the same time continue their Jewish life and culture on what was for them their historic soil.

But the situation changed after the Communist Revolution of 1917. The communist leaders of the Soviet Union regarded all movements of racial and religious hate as being against the best interests of the country. They characterized them as weapons manipulated by the propertied and privileged classes in their drive to maintain their control over the government for the purpose of protecting their wealth and power. The Soviet government therefore prohibited racial and religious hatred, including anti-Semitism, by declaring such activities to be crimes against the Soviet system. The Soviet courts enforced the laws against anti-Semitism, and a well-organized educational campaign was undertaken throughout the country to teach the people to respect the cultural rights of all minority peoples.

The Soviet leaders fostered cultural activity among all the national groups within the country. The czars, on the other hand, had oppressed many of the non-Russian national groups; they had tried to Russianize the various nationalities by forcing them to give up their centuries-old customs, languages, folkways, and religious beliefs.

Years of such czarist rule had caused a number of ancient languages to disappear. Although people spoke those languages in their homes, the schools were not permitted to teach them and very little writing was done in them. The culture that had been developed in those tongues also began to disappear. The Soviet Union, believing that true equality and friendship among the varied peoples of the country could come about only when each was free to continue and develop the best in its cultural past, sent scholars to the various nationalities to revive their ancient languages. These tongues were made the language of instruction in the local schools, and newspapers and printing presses were set up by which these nations could popularize their cultures. The U.S.S.R. also established special museums to acquaint the different peoples with the customs and folkways, the art and literature, as well as the handicrafts and other products that each group had contributed to the general progress and well-being of the country.

For the Jews, the Soviet government developed a special program as well. Because the czars had denied them the right to engage extensively in farming, large sections in Byelo-Russia, the Ukraine, and the Crimea were set aside as Jewish farming regions. With great excitement, and in a pioneering spirit no less zealous than that of the Jews in Palestine, thousands of Jewish families streamed toward these areas. The hardships they encountered were of little moment to them, because they felt that now, at last, they belonged, that they could help build up a land in which they were completely accepted. By 1938, more than two hundred and fifty thousand Jews were on the land, in thriving agricultural communities. And since the agricultural system in the Soviet Union was based on the principle of co-operative, collective farming, the Jewish farm communities were also collectives, not unlike the co-operatives of Palestine.

The Soviets also sought to satisfy the age-old longing of the Russian Jews for a place in the sun—for statehood and national life. In 1928 the government set aside Biro-Bidjan, in the Soviet Far East near Manchuria and Vladivostok, as a Jewish district, for settlement by those Jews who wished to develop a Jewish state within the Soviet Union. In 1934 Biro-Bidjan was designated an autonomous region, a step away from being recognized as a Jewish autonomous republic. There, the Jewish settlers enjoy full self-government, having the power to make and enforce laws for the regulation of life in their region. The Jews of Biro-Bidjan elect their own officials, and are represented in the Council of Nationalities of the U.S.S.R., like our U.S. Senate, as a Jewish nation within the Soviet Union. Jews, like all other peoples in the Soviet Union, are represented in the government as individuals and as members of a national group.

By 1946 the population of Biro-Bidjan was estimated at 175,000, of which 115,000 were Jews. Had such a state been established in the time of the czars, many hundreds of thousands more would probably have flocked to it, to escape discrimination and anti-Semitism. But under the Soviets every Jew enjoyed full equality as an individual; he was not discriminated against in school or government, farm, or factory because of racial, religious, or national reasons. Jews no longer felt the need to seek special protection as Jews. There was, therefore, no general exodus of Jews from the European section of the Soviet Union to Biro-Bidjan. Those who did go there did so largely because of their Jewish national feeling—they wanted to build a Jewish state, to realize their ambition for a truly national existence, on an equal basis with the other peoples of the Soviet Union.

There are a number of differences between the Jewish national life in Israel and Jewish nationalism in the Soviet Union. In Israel, the official national language of the Jews is Hebrew, in Biro-Bidjan it is Yiddish. The Jews of Israel are completely independent, free to organize their life as they see fit. In Biro-Bidjan the Jews are not completely on their own: they can develop their culture as they wish, but their economic system must fit in with the plans and methods of the government of the Soviet Union.

Even the cultural outlook of the Jews of Israel is different. The Jews who live there came from many lands. They brought to it ideas and skills, interests and attitudes which they had developed in the several countries of their origin. They are gradually merging these backgrounds, and are creating a national culture based on their present experiences in Palestine, as well as on their past association with it. For example, certain traditional religious observances, such as the Jewish Sabbath and the ancient Hebrew Sukkoth and Hanukkah festivals, are becoming national, as well as religious, holidays, and their observance has taken entirely new forms and expressions.

The culture of the Jews of the Soviet Union has developed along different lines. Since the Soviet Union for a long time discouraged religious observance, whether Jewish, Christian, or Mohammedan, Jewish religious traditions have played a minor part in their life. Soviet Jewish folkways have been influenced by their experiences under Soviet rule and by the customs that developed in the European ghettos more than by echoes from their Hebrew past. Many of the Jewish folk songs from the Soviet Union, for instance, deal with pioneer life in the Jewish collective farms and in Biro-Bidjan, and express the enthusiasm of the Jews for the work they are doing as builders of a new life. They do not contain religious overtones, nor the note of sadness that had crept into Jewish songs in the days of their oppression.

Jewish culture in the Soviet Union is based on a warm regard for their life in the past, particularly their history in Russia, and stresses those accomplishments and folk feelings that are in keeping with the spirit of the country they live in. Many of the Soviet Jewish national events come from their Russian past, rather than from their existence as a religious community, as for example, the celebration of the anniversary of Sholom Aleichem, the great Yiddish writer. They also celebrate various Soviet national holidays and occasions, since they are an integral part of the Soviet Union.

The primary loyalty of the Jews in Israel is to their own land; their primary cultural affiliation is to Jewish life. In the Soviet Union, the Jews, like all other Soviet peoples, have dual identification; as a national group and as citizens of the Soviet Union.

These two Jewish communities, therefore, represent two worlds of Jewish life and endeavor; in Israel, a nation enjoying an independent national existence, and in the Soviet Union, a national body among many other ethnic and national groups.

But most of the Jews live outside these two areas, in still another kind of world. There are Jews in England, France, the Scandinavian countries, Holland, Belgium, Italy, Poland, Romania, in fact, in practically every country of Europe. In the Western Hemisphere they are found in Canada, the United States, Mexico, Argentina, and many other Latin-American countries. There are Jews in Egypt, Iran, Iraq, and other Moslem lands. Their existence as Jews in these countries is quite different from the Jewish life in Israel and the Soviet Union. Jewish life in the United States, while it differs in many details from the kind of life Jews live in the countries outside Israel and the Soviet Union, contains a great many features common to all of them.

It is most important to note the fact that anti-Jewishness did not become a part of national policy in the United States. It never became as much a part of the American culture pattern as in European lands. Washington, Jefferson, Thomas Paine, and the other revolutionary leaders set out to make true democracy work; and the Bill of Rights expressly forbade the establishment of any faith as the official religion of the United States. Moreover, America had tremendous stretches of land available for its growing population and many opportunities for a livelihood for those willing to work. Therefore, the element of economic competition of Jews was absent in America in the early years of the nation, and Jews were welcomed as contributors to its development.

Jews were therefore accepted as an integral part of the country from colonial times. Citizenship was not conferred on them in a grudging sort of way as in European countries. From the very outset they held American citizenship by birth and naturalization like all other Americans, and enjoyed the rights and privileges guaranteed by the Constitution to all citizens. There were no preferred groups, as in the nationalistic countries of Europe. In America it was the individual who counted; citizenship was not restricted to people of certain religious faiths or national origins.

Under such a democratic system the Jews developed a completely American outlook. Their mother tongue became English; they took part in every American activity, in business, politics, and sports. Jewish writers and artists dealt with American subjects. While their grandfathers had spent their lives mastering the law, philosophy, and history of the Jews in Biblical and ghetto times, American Jews concentrated on the law, philosophy, and history of the American people, of which they felt themselves joyfully a part. America was their homeland, American culture their culture.

American Jews, especially before the 1880's and 1890's, identified themselves with the Jewish fold mainly through their religion. Those Jews who strayed from the religious practices of their parents felt only a vague sense of being Jewish, especially since the separation of Church and State in America made it unnecessary for any person to register his religious affiliation. Religion was a person's private concern, a matter for his own conscience or feeling to decide.

Most of the Jews voluntarily decided to continue some aspect of Jewish tradition. Orthodox, Conservative, and Reform congregations were organized wherever Jews congregated. Hebrew schools, seminaries, and Sunday schools were maintained; fraternal organizations were formed for social and philanthropic purposes; and there were also societies that kept alive the cultural bonds with the past by publishing Jewish newspapers and books in English, Yiddish, and Hebrew. But Jewish interests and cultural expression were definitely subordinated to their lives as Americans.

After the 1880's, when large numbers of Jews started to

come to America from eastern Europe, a change in Jewish outlook began to take place. The Russian, Polish, and other East-European Jews brought with them a highly developed Jewish consciousness, born of their folk experiences in those lands. They brought a Jewish culture, largely influenced by the Haskalah movement and the Yiddish language. Yiddish newspapers were established, a number of Yiddish theaters were organized in New York, where large numbers of Jews had settled, and companies of actors, dancers, singers, and musicians toured America to present Jewish programs in various communities. Talmud Torahs, Yeshivahs, and other institutions of Jewish studies sprang up; Jewish life in America experienced a new birth, in the pattern of the life and interests of the Jews of eastern Europe, who were now becoming the dominant element in the Jewish population in the cities of America.

During this period of large-scale immigration to America, the descendants of other national groups that had settled in America also experienced a revival of interest in the Old World culture of their ancestors. Germans, Scandinavians, Italians, Greeks, Russians, and others developed a new interest in the folkways of their people, as the immigrants brought with them the sound and breath of the "old country."

But the American emphasis on individual liberty, and the lack of official discrimination against any group, served to weaken the ties to the Old World cultures as time went by. As the children went through American schools and colleges; as they participated in American sports and forms of recreation and celebrated American national holidays, they identified themselves more and more with the tra-

ditions of American life; and the folkways of their foreign-
born parents became less and less a part of their lives.

Jews as well as Gentiles began to accept the "melting-
pot" idea—that people should adapt themselves to American
life and give up their affiliation to "foreign" customs and
folkways. American life was so free there was no need to
bother with speaking and reading the mother tongue—
everyone was learning to speak and read English. And so,
as the second and third generations became more "Americanized" there was a general falling off of interest in the
"old country" culture among the descendants of the immigrants from European nations.

In the same way, Jewish cultural activity also entered a
period of decline, particularly in the 1920's, when large-
scale Jewish immigration from eastern Europe ended. The
Russian Revolution, out of which came the Soviet Union,
cut down the number who sought to emigrate from that
country, and American immigration restrictions cut down
the number who could enter the United States from East-
European or other lands. No new waves of Jewish immigration flowed into the country to revive interest in the old
customs. American Jewish cultural activity had to depend
now upon the Jews who were already in the country, most
of whom had become quite thoroughly Americanized.

Meanwhile, many social and economic changes were
occurring in the United States. The government no longer
had free land in the West to open up to settlers; the country was being rapidly industrialized, bringing in its train
a series of depressions—in 1873, 1884, 1893, 1907, 1921,
1929. Moreover, as a result of the growth of large corporations and chain stores, the opportunities for inde-

pendent, small business were being cut down. The union movement grew rapidly, and a struggle began between management and labor for control of the government.

All of these developments resulted in a situation in which racial, religious, and nationalist hatreds could be used by various groups to maintain their established positions, just as these hatreds had been employed to that end in European countries.

When unemployment and hard times made many people feel insecure and discontented, various minority groups were singled out for attack. In some sections of the country, the immigrants were accused of taking away the jobs of Americans. In some sections the discontent was directed against the Negro, in some against the Chinese and Japanese; in still others against Mexicans, Hungarians, Poles—whatever group could be used as a "bogyman" with which to frighten people. The Jews were also attacked.

First and second generation American Jews soon began to feel the effects of the propaganda campaigns against them. They were called "hyphenated Americans" for being interested in the customs and culture of their Old World origins and in the welfare of their fellow Jews in those lands. Foreign-sounding names became, for sensitive children of immigrant families, a source of embarrassment. Jews and non-Jews began to change their names, to make them more American sounding. Many Jews and non-Jews turned away from the cultural interests of their parents and grandparents altogether, in their eagerness to become as "American" as possible.

On the other hand, large numbers began to resist this tendency. They insisted on their right as Americans to participate in whatever cultural activities they held dear, so long as they did not violate the spirit of American democracy. American culture itself, they pointed out, had developed from the cultural strains that settlers of foreign origin had brought to these shores in every period of American history. The melting-pot idea was all wrong, they maintained—cultural differences should not be boiled away, even if it were possible thus to eradicate them from people's lives, since it made for a more colorful life when a country had varied customs and folkways; it was far more interesting than to have a monotonous sameness wherever anyone turned. Thus, in practically every group of foreign origin in the country, including the Jews, there were those who took steps deliberately to keep alive the old culture, while the believers in the melting-pot idea strayed further and further from the customs and traditions of their parents and grandparents.

Besides being disturbed by the anti-foreign propaganda, the Jews also felt the hostility resulting from the rise of anti-Semitism in America. Some of it was brought here by European immigrants who had been infected by the germ. Much of it, however, grew up right within the country, as part of the heritage of European civilization that the early settlers had brought to the New World. The sickness had been kept from becoming epidemic because of the democratic scheme of American life, coupled with the economic opportunities America offered during the years of its amazing expansion. Slowly, however, the latent anti-Jewishness began to emerge, as hate-mongering agents concentrated their attention on the Jews in periods of crisis and hard times.

In the 1930's, the native anti-Semitic leaders received the support of the Hitlerites here and abroad. The success the Nazis had achieved through the use of anti-Semitism, encouraged the power-mad, would-be Hitlers in America. For there were some Americans who actually hoped that the liberal, democratic spirit in the United States would be weakened by the turmoil and agitation of the anti-Semitic movement; they, like the financiers and industrialists in Hitler Germany, gave financial and moral support to the hate-mongers.

The movement received a serious setback during the Second World War. However, the anti-Semites did not give up; they simply bided their time, and came to life again in the period after the war. Fortunately, the democratic idea is deeply ingrained in American civilization and law; large numbers of Americans of all faiths are opposed to anti-Semitism and are actively engaged in fighting it. Time alone will tell how healthy and strong the principles of the Declaration of Independence and the Bill of Rights are, for the anti-Semites have by no means given up their activities. So long as prejudice against Jews still exists in employment practices, in clubs, in certain residential sections, in schools and colleges, and in many social activities, the professional anti-Semites will be able to ply their trade. And they will find support among those groups who will stoop to any means to perpetuate their position or power.

Meanwhile, the anti-Semitic propaganda has had its effects upon Jews. Many colleges, particularly medical schools, maintained a quota system to restrict the number of Jewish students they admitted. Many firms refused to hire Jewish workers or professionals. Many hotels barred

Jews, and special clauses were written into some real estate contracts to keep Jews out of certain localities. As in Europe, this evidence of hostility caused among Jews a sense of unease, of insecurity; it began to color their thought and outlook.

A good deal of Jewish communal activity was taken up by the active fight against these various manifestations of anti-Semitism. Many Jews, like those who had assimilated into western European culture, began to wonder just what it meant to be a Jew; now that they were made conscious of the fact that they were being identified in the popular mind as Jews, they sought to understand the place of Jewishness in the American scene.

There are American Jews who find the hostile climate too difficult to live in; they have come to regard Jewishness as a "state of mind," an identification that a person is free to accept or reject depending on his own point of view. They think of themselves as simply Americans; and since they have no interest in the religion of Judaism or the traditions and folkways of the Jews, they resent the label society has pinned on them. Such Jews represent only a small section of the Jewish population in America.

By far the greatest number of American Jews think of Jewish life in terms of religion, as symbolized by the synagogue or temple. They see no conflict between their Jewishness and Americanism—they are like Catholic or Protestant Americans who follow certain practices and ceremonials that have come out of their religious beliefs.

A fairly large number of Jews, however, like their Christian neighbors, are no longer consciously inspired by religious motives. They are not affiliated with congregations and do not observe religious Holy Days or ceremonials. Neither do they have a uniform approach to, or sense of identification with, the Jewish community in America or abroad. Some are Yiddishists, who respond to the culture the Jew created in that language. Others, who are not interested in Yiddish or Hebrew as a language, nevertheless feel a sentimental attachment to Jewish life—to the literature, customs, music, and other cultural developments that were part of the Jewishness of their parents or grandparents.

Like other people in American life who are linked by religion, or common historical experience, or language and customs, the Jews also constitute a more or less cohesive group. They do not have a uniform pattern of life that marks them off as Jewish; like other peoples, they neither think alike nor act alike, nor do they all to the same extent enjoy or participate in the cultural life of their particular group. They simply share certain experiences of the past, voluntarily identifying themselves, on an individual basis, with those aspects of the common cultural heritage that please them. Like the others, too, their Jewish identification is secondary; their primary attachment is to America as their homeland; to its national observances, its forms of community and family life, its ways of work and recreation.

The Jews in Israel, on the other hand, constitute an actual nation, politically, socially, and economically. Their outlook and culture are completely, and consciously, Jewish.

The Jews of the Soviet Union comprise a national group within a multi-national country. Their culture is not religious; but it is Jewish in the sense that the values they cherish arose from the distinctive customs, outlook, and folkways that had developed among them in the pre-Soviet Jewish communities of Russia. But they are citizens of the Soviet Union; and as such, especially in Biro-Bidjan, they are like the other nationalities in the Soviet Union, who, while continuing the traditions of the past, also participate in the Soviet culture that has been developing since 1917.

In ancient Palestine and in the ghettos, Jewishness was a way of life, a pattern of existence for each Jew in the community. He lived under the divine authority of the Torah and its traditional, religious regulations which governed every aspect of the individual's life within the Jewish community. Today, most Jews do not live in compact communities where this kind of Jewishness suffuses the very atmosphere they live in. The meaning of "Jewishness" is today interpreted in various ways. To some, Jewishness is an identification with the culture of the Jewish past, sometimes including the religious, and sometimes excluding it. To others it consists of a sense of obligation to, and participation in, organized community life, such as the support of Jewish philanthropies. To some Jews, it is nothing more than a sympathetic feeling toward people who, like themselves, happened to be born of Jewish parents. To most Jews, however, it means positive affiliation with the Jewish religion through membership in a synagogue.

It is a remarkable achievement for a people to have continued for so long a period in history as have the Jews, for many a people and nation whose exploits fill pages in the histories of ancient civilization no longer exist. Unlike these, the Jews have not disappeared; they have continued on, developing along the way a rich culture which still gives warmth and sustenance to millions of Jews. Out of their life and literature—out of their Torah—have come moral and ethical teachings which have become part of the civilization of the Western World.

What new values will come out of the reconstituted Jewish commonwealth in Israel, or from the new form of Jewish life in the Soviet Union, or from the complex and complicated Jewish community of America, cannot be predicted. What form Judaism will take in the future and how Jewish life will express itself, will be determined to a large extent, as it was in the past, by the play of the social forces of those lands where Jews will be found.

Jews have lived through times that have seen finis written on the pages of history for other peoples. Throughout those periods they kept alive the traditions of their past, taking them along as precious baggage whenever history sent them traveling; and these traditions held them firmly together as a people. Always they developed new patterns of life as historical forces played upon them, just as they are now creating new forms of Jewish life to fit modern society. This, too, is part of the tradition that has kept the Jews alive; for their religion and social ideals, stemming from the Prophets of Israel, were not fixed and immutable, but rather guides for purposeful living. For this reason Jews will continue to live as long as man's spirit reaches toward the realization of the Prophetic ideals of justice, democracy, and peace.

GUIDE TO PRONUNCIATION

(In the following phonetic transliteration *ch* has the sound
of *ch* in German *ach*.)

Aleichem (ah-lay-chem')
Antigonus (an-tig'-o-nus)
Antiochus (an-tie'-o-kus)
Antipas (an'-tih-pas)
Antipater (an-tip'-uh-ter)
Avicebron (ah-vee-seb'-ron)
Baal Shem Tob (bah'-ahl-shame-tove)
Bet Ha-midrash (bate ha-mid'-rahsh)
Calas (kah-lah')
Epiphanes (ee-pif'-uh-neez)
Esdraelon (ez-dree'-lon)
Exilarch (ex'-i-lark)
Gabirol (gah-bee'-rol)
Gaonim (gay-oh'neem)
Haganah (hah-gah-nah')
Haggai (hah'-guy)
Hammurabi (hah-moor-ah'-bee)
Hannukkah (chah'-noo-kah)
Hasidim (chah-see'-dim)
Haskalah (hahs-kah'-lah)
Hasmoneans (haz-mo-nee'-ans)
Haym (chah'-yim)
Hosea (hoh-zay'-uh)
Isaiah (eye-zay'-uh)
Israeli (iz-rah-ay'-lee)
Jahweh (yah'-weh)
Jeremiah (jer-uh-my'-uh)
Jeroboam (je-ruh-bow'-am)
Johanan (yo'-cha-nahn)
Johann (yo'-hahn)

Jonadab (yo'-na-dab)
Josiah (joh-zeye'-uh)
Judah Halevi (joo'-dah ha-lay'-vee)
Judaism (joo'-dah-izm)
Maimonides (my-mon'-uh-deez)
Mattathias (mat-tah-thy'-us)
Menelaus (men-uh-lay'-us)
Nebuchadnezzar (neh-boo-chad-nez'-er)
Nehemiah (nee-huh-my'-uh)
Pentateuch (pen'-tah-tooch)
Pesach (pay'-sahch)
Pontius (pon'-shus)
Rechabites (rech'-uh-bites)
Reuchlin (roy'-chlin)
Saadiah (sah'-dyuh)
Schulchan Aruch (shool'-chun ah'-rooch)
Seder (say'der)
Seixas (say'shus)
Shabbatai Zevi (shah'-bah-tie tsvee)
Sholom (shahl-ohm')
Sukkoth (sook'-oht)
Talmud (tahl'-mood)
Tishah B'Ab (tish'-ah b-ahv')
Torah (toe'-rah)
Zechariah (zehchah-rye'-uh)
Zeus (zoos)
Zerubbabel (ze-roo'-ba-vel)

GLOSSARY

B.C. AND A.D.: When writing for a Jewish public under Jewish sponsorship, the Jewish historian uses the abbreviation "C.E." (the Common Era) instead of "A.D." This is done because of theological objection to A.D., which means "in the year of the Lord." For the same reason he uses "B.C.E." (Before the Common Era) instead of "B.C.," which stands for "Before Christ," since in Jewish theology Jesus is not recognized as the Lord or the Christ (derived from "Christos," the Greek translation of the Hebrew word for Messiah).

BAAL WORSHIP: When the seminomadic Hebrews entered Canaan they learned to live as farmers, adopting many of the customs and folkways of the native Canaanite population, especially their religious practices. When the Hebrews used the Canaanite rites in the worship of their own god, Jahweh, this practice was referred to by the prophets as Baal worship. To them it meant that the Hebrews were actually worshiping the Baals, the local Canaanite deities, and not Jahweh, their own god.

ETHICAL MONOTHEISM: The belief in one God, whose nature is moral. In the worship of such a God, therefore, it is required that people observe a moral code in their personal lives and in their relations with others.

EXILE: Refers to the period after 586 B.C., when the Jews were held captive in Babylon. The period of exile ends

Glossary

about 420 B.C., when the second Jewish commonwealth in Palestine was established.

GENTILES: Derived from "gens," the Latin translation of the Hebrew word "Goy," which means a nation, or a community. All non-Jewish peoples were referred to as "Goyyim." Thus, "Gentiles" when used in Jewish literature refers to non-Jews.

GOD-OF-THE-LAND: The Canaanites believed that their gods, or Baals, lived in certain localities and were effective only in those places. The Hebrews, before the Exile, believed that their god, Jahweh, was the god of Palestine and could be worshiped only on the soil of that land. Thus, Jahweh, as well as the Baals, were local gods—"gods-of-the-land"—only. The Prophets, in opposition to this popular conception, conceived of Jahweh as a Universal God, who could be worshiped by any people in any land.

HOLY WAFERS: This is the name given to the bread used in the ceremony of communion, which, according to Catholic doctrine, is changed after the Act of Consecration, into the body of Jesus.

ISRAELITES: The Hebrews who inhabited the ancient, northern kingdom of Israel, were called Israelites. The term is also used to denote the ancient Hebrew people in general, who are referred to as *B'nai Yisroel*, the children of Israel. The inhabitants of the new republic of Israel are called "Israelis" (Iz-rah-ay-lees).

Glossary

MYSTERY RELIGIONS: A term applied to certain religious societies in the Graeco-Roman world, which required their devotees to undergo special initiation ceremonies and to observe certain secret practices and teachings which they were not permitted to reveal. These "mysteries" were attractive to vast numbers of people because they offered satisfaction to the hope for "salvation": that is, personal communion with a deity who was interested in them and their affairs, and who would support them in time of trial during their lives and receive them lovingly in the world beyond the grave.

ORAL LAW: Those traditional laws of Judaism which are not contained in the Pentateuch itself. The Pharisaic teachers taught that, in addition to the Written Law, there was an Oral Law, representing the interpretations by which the Torah was adapted to new conditions of life. These interpretations of the Written Law were collected and edited by Judah Hanasi as the Mishnah; still later, the Mishnah and the new interpretations of it were collected and edited into a code which is known as the Talmud. This Oral Law was looked upon as the word of God no less than the Written Law, since each new interpretation was derived from the Torah. (See WRITTEN LAW.)

PENTATEUCH: The first five books of the Hebrew Bible, or "Old Testament" (Genesis, Exodus, Leviticus, Numbers, and Deuteronomy.)

PROPHETS: As used in this book, the term "Prophets" refers to such men as Elijah, Amos, Hosea, Micah, Isaiah, Jeremiah, and Ezekiel, who looked upon themselves as ambassadors of God, commissioned to make known His will and purpose to His people. They were essentially preachers and teachers of religion.

SANHEDRIN: In general, this term applies to the court which interpreted the Jewish law and traditions and enacted decrees for religious observance. It was composed of seventy-one members at first, and later only seventy.

SEMITES: Those peoples who were reputedly descended from Shem, the son of Noah. However, in modern times, the term is applied to those peoples who speak the related group of tongues known as "Semitic languages," among which are the Assyrian, Babylonian, Hebrew, Arabic, and others.

In the nineteenth century, certain anthropologists attributed racial characteristics to the people who spoke the Semitic languages, as they did also to those who spoke the Indo-European, or Aryan, languages.

The idea that there are Semitic and Aryan races has been proven fallacious by modern anthropologists. Yet the myth persists that the Semitic peoples are inferior to the Aryans, to whom certain writers had attributed all the ideal and acceptable virtues, in contrast to the Semites, to whom were attributed all the vices.

SHULCHAN ARUCH: The code containing the laws of Orthodox Judaism; they regulate every phase of Jewish life and are based on the traditions of the past.

The term, translated literally, means "the prepared table,"

for it was meant to make it possible for anyone to make decisions in all problems of Jewish law with the same ease with which he helps himself to food from a table already prepared for a meal.

THEOCRACY: That form of government that recognizes God as ruler, or king; a state governed by laws that are believed to be issued by God, and which laws are interpreted by those who are accepted as the agents and representatives of God.

WRITTEN LAW: The commandments *written* in the five books of Moses (the Pentateuch), governing individual and social conduct, and ritual and ceremonial observance. According to the Orthodox Jewish tradition they were *written* by Moses at the dictation of God at Mt. Sinai. (See ORAL LAW.)

INDEX

Page numbers in italics indicate that the word is defined in the Glossary.

Index

115; Council of Nicaea, 115–
116; Crusades against Islam,
136–141; dominant force in
Middle Ages, 143–144; injunc-
tion against fraternization
with Jews, 129–132, 134; as
landowner, 129, 164; part in
Mortara incident, 188–189;
persecution of Jews, 129–134;
role in political affairs, 164–
165, 227
Ceremonies, religious: 3–5, 44–
45, 62
Charities, Jewish: 153, 242, 262
Chasidim: 173
Christian(s): acceptance of Jewish neighbors, 130, 179; animosity against Jews, 102, 116
131, 181; Bible adopted officially, 115; Gentiles converted
by Paul, 101–103; origin as
Judaeo-Christians, 99, 127;
outside fold of Judaism, 108–
109; persecution as heretics,
129, 143–145; persecution of
Jews by, 138–139, 180; victims
of Roman persecution, 128
Christianity: acknowledged as
Gentile sect, 109; adoption of
Christian Bible, 107–108, 115;
belief in Day of Judgment,
99; differentiated from Judaeo-Christians, 99–100; divided into Catholic and Protestant sects, 166–168; indebted
to Jewish scholars, 155–156;
principles enunciated by Jesus,
95–97; as religion of Roman
empire, 128
Circumcision: 58–59, 100, 109
Commonwealth, Jewish: 56–58,
64, 69, 81

Communion: 102
Co-operatives: 243, 249
Covenant: 10–11, 19, 28–33, 41,
48, 57–58
Creation of man, literature of:
59–60, 155
Crusades: 126, 136–141, 150
Customs (implied in Hebrew
Covenant): fallow fields for
poor, 41; freedom from usury
for poor, 41; inalienable ownership of land, 29–30, 46;
mortgaging and foreclosing
forbidden, 32, 41, 46
Cyrus the Great: 63–64

David, King: 16–21
David, House of: 21, 40, 56, 83
Day of Judgment: 71, 93–94, 99
Deborah: 13–14
Democracy: ideals arising in
French Revolution, 177–185;
ideals outlined by Prophets,
53–54; influence weakened by
nationalism, 231–233; in mod-
ern Israel, 243; liberal ideas
introduced in 19th century,
226
Deuteronomic Code: 45–46
Dietary laws: 63, 74, 78, 100, 222
Divided kingdoms: period of,
26–42
Dreyfus case: 231–233, 237

Edict of Toleration: 180
Education: academies in Palestine, 109–110; first law for
compulsory, 85; in ghetto
years, 156; in hands of Catholic Church, 131; permitted
under Mohammedans, 120; in
Persian community, 112–113;
synagogue's part in, 85

Index

pean countries, 148; admitted
to Russia, 196–197; attacked
by Christians, 102; attitude
toward religion today, 260;
banned from England, 218;
cancellation of debts to, 140;
in colonial America, 202–208;
contributions to knowledge,
156, 159; emancipation from
ghetto life, 163–187, 190–191;
emigration to United States,
198, 204–206, 211, 213–214; expulsion during 13th-15th centuries, 142; forced to pay for
protection, 135–136; granted
citizenship rights, 178, 186–
187, 190–191, 201, 205, 253; in
Grecian world, 72–80; Hellenized group of, 75; life in
ghettos, 149–162; life in Pale
of Settlement, 193–194, 200;
massacred during Crusades,
138–139; as minority group in
Russia, 197–201; in modern
Palestine, 237, 242–247, 261–
262; under Mohammedan rule,
119–126; Persian communities,
61–64, 66, 111–114; rebellion
under Maccabees, 79–81; scattering after Roman defeat,
105; self-government under
Persians, 63–70; in Soviet Russia, 237, 247–252, 261–263; unrest under Roman rule, 85–
110; in United States, 209–214,
237, 253–261, 263; wide modern distribution, 252
Jewish commonwealth: establishment of, 64–69; high priest
as leader of, 81; planned by
Ezekiel, 56–58; struggle by
Pharisees for ethical values in,
92

Jewish nation. *See* Israel (mod-
ern nation)
Jezebel: 30–31
Johanan ben Zakkai: 106–108
John the Baptist: 94–95
John Hyrcanus: 83
Jonadab ben Rechab: 33
Jonathan (son of Saul): 16–17
Jonathan (brother of Judah
Maccabee): 81
Joram: 32
Jordan River: 31, 94
Joseph: 7
Joshua: 12
Josiah: 45–46
Judaeo-Christians: 99, 216
Judah, kingdom of: adoption of
Assyrian rituals, 44–45; af-
flicted by social ills, 43; flight
of Israelites to, 43; kingdom
destroyed by Babylonians,
47–50; organization of king-
dom, 17; separation from
Israel, 26; union with Israel,
18; wars after separation, 27
Judah Halevi: 122, 154–156
Judah Hanasi: 110, 267
Judah Maccabee: 78
Judaism: belief in angels, 71;
Conservative, 225, 254; effort
to modernize, 222–225; idea of
immortality, 71; Karaism as
sect of, 123, 124; man's relationship to God in, 71; nar-
rowed down by Shulchan
Aruch, 157; new form of religion, 69; Orthodox, 225, 254,
267; phases emphasized by
prophets in Exile, 62–63; Reform, 223–225, 254; as rival of
Christianity, 102, 105, 216–217;
superiority to other faiths,
125; war on, by Romans, 99,

Index

Nazis: 234–235
Nebuchadnezzar: 47–49
Nehemiah: 67–69
New Testament: 115
Nomads: 2–5
Nones, Benjamin: 208, 210–211

Occupations (of Jews): agriculture difficult under Catholic Church, 132–133; in Babylon, 111; banking (moneylending), 134, 136, 215, 219; competition by Christians, 136–142, 145; guilds closed to Jews, 134; trade, 135–136; in modern times, 190, 242, 249; peddling, 134; in Russia, 196–197, 249
Oral Law: *267;* codification into Mishnah, 110; discarded by Karaites, 123; as "fence around Torah," 74–75; insistence of Pharisees on, 83; recorded as Talmud, 114

Pale of Settlement: 193–194, 200, 247
Palestine: decline of Jews in, 110; importance of trade routes through, 1, 14; influence of commercial economy upon Hebrews, 28–30, 33; modern Jewish state in, *see* Israel (modern nation); name derived from Philistines, 14; people carried to Exile from, 50; return to, after Exile, 63–65; return to, under Joshua, 12; self-government in, under Greeks, 80–84; self-government in, under Persians, 70; settlement by first Hebrew tribe, 6–7
Passover: 96, 153, 219

Paul (or Saul): 99–102
Pentateuch: 60, *267*
Persecution (of Jews): banned from certain countries, 142, 147, 218; by Catholic Church, 129–134; forced to live in ghettos, 149–150; under Inquisition, 145–148; in Middle Ages, 138–141, 217–219; by Mohammedans, 126; by Persians, 113–114; by Rome, 103–105, 116. *Also see* Anti-Semitism
Persians: 63–72, 89
Pesach (Passover): 96, 153, 219
Pharisees: 82–86, 91, 104
Philistines: 14–18
Philosophy: Greek, 122; ideas of Locke, Rousseau, Voltaire, 168–170; Jewish contributions to, 155–156
Pogroms: 195, 198
Pompey: 85–86
Pontius Pilate: 95–98
Prophets: 35–41, 44–49, 169, 242, 243, *267–268;* prophetic books declared sacred, 107; significance of, 51–54; struggle for social justice, 34–50. *Also see* Amos, Elijah, Ezekiel, Hosea, both Isaiahs, Jeremiah, Micah
Protestantism: 160, 166–172, 205, 219–220
Purim: 153

Rechabites: 33
Red Sea: 9
Reform Judaism: 223–225
Rehoboam: 24–26
Reuchlin, Johann: 166
Revolution: American, 176–177, 206–208; events leading up to Russian, 192–197; French,

GREECE

CYPRUS

MEDITERRANEAN SEA

SYRIA

PHOENICIA

Sidon
Tyre
Damascus

ISRAEL
Samaria
PHILISTIA
Jerusalem
JUDAH
MOAB
NEGEB
AMMON

ARABIA

Euf

Cairo

EGYPT

SINAI PENINSULA

NileRiver

RED SEA

Haifa
Tel Aviv
ISRAEL
Jerusalem
NEGEB
TRANSJORDAN

Scale of Miles
50   0   50   100   150

THE FERTILE CRESCE